MW00697522

Simple Rules to Ace the ACT/English and SAT/Writing Sections

KILLER
ACT/SAT GRAMMAR

TOM CLEMENTS

HIT 'EM UP PUBLISHING
CALIFORNIA 2016

TC TUTORING — Download my free "Killer SAT Grammar" app from the App store.

Copyright 2016 by Tom Clements

All rights reserved. Except as permitted under the U.S. Copyright Act of 1976,
no part of this publication may be reproduced, distributed, or
transmitted in any form or by any means, or stored in a database or retrieval system,
without the prior written permission of the publisher.

TC TUTORING
346 Rheem Blvd, Suite 110-B
Moraga, California, 94556
www.tctutoring.net

First Edition: December 2016

Cover design by Namita Kapoor

Special thanks to Sumi Clements and Caie Kelly

Printed in the United States of America
ISBN: 978-0-692-79286-5

Table of Contents

copyright © 2016

copyright © 2016

copyright © 2016

Part I Rules

≡

1—Apostrophes

Short and sweet, this section reviews the rules for apostrophes on both the SAT and ACT tests.

Possession

1) Singular Possession

Use apostrophes in order to indicate possession of an item with a singular noun. (*Person, Place, or thing or idea*)
For example:

> *The water bottle's cap*   Anuka's Car
>
> *Susan's arm*   Bob's

When a singular noun ends with an "s", you will still add "s" to show ownership. For example, *The Hawkins's house* or *Kansas's corn*. Weird, but correct.

2) Plural Possession

When a plural noun ends in "s" simply add an apostrophe to the end. For example:

> *The parents' car*   The boys' basketball
>
> *The families' vacations*   The goys' trucks
>
> *The girls' group*

When the plural noun doesn't end in "s," add "s" to create the possessive:

> *The children's fireplace*

Note: For plural possessive **pronouns** (my, our, his, hers, its, yours, theirs), **do not** add an apostrophe — especially no apostrophe for *its*!

≡

Contractions

Apostrophes can also be used to show that a word has been shortened. No biggie:

They have > they've

She will > she'll

Will not > won't

It is > It's

Note: *It's* is the correct verb-form contraction. As mentioned on the previous page, there is no such thing as *its'* in English. The ONLY two forms are:

*The dog ate **its** food. **It's** time to go.*

***NEVER**: The dog ate **its'** food. **Its** time to go.*

Practice Q&A

Working through these practice questions with follow-up explanations will help you put all of these comma rules into action. As they say, practice makes perfect.

1) Before 8000 BC, <u>humanitys' food</u> came almost exclusively from hunting and gathering.

    A. no change

    B. humanity's food

    C. humanities' food

    D. foods' of humanity

The correct answer is B. Although "humanity" is talking about a large group, the word itself encompasses all of the humans in the world, and therefore the word does not become "humanities" in the context of this sentence.

2) <u>Athletic human's</u> daily consumption are much more than the average human being.

    A. no change

    B. athletic humans

    C. athletic humans'

    D. human's athletic

Begin by focusing only on the word "human." Here, the author seems to be talking about multiple humans, which is a hint that the current construction is incorrect. We need to make humans plural and then simply add an apostrophe to the end to make the word possessive, so C is the correct answer.

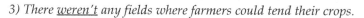

3) There <u>weren't</u> any fields where farmers could tend their crops.

A. no change

B. wer'nt

C. were are not

D. werent'

The correct answer is A. Remember that when contracting two words together, an apostrophe is placed in the space where the letter was before. In this case, "were not" contracts to "weren't."

4) According to <u>paleontologists' accounts</u>, life for prehistoric humans was difficult.

A. no change

B. paleontologist's accounts

C. accounts by paleontologists'

D. paleontologists accounts

Here, we begin by making the word "paleontologist" plural, and then simply add an apostrophe to the end. The original grammatical construction is correct, and the answer is A.

5) Some of the seeds dropped out of the <u>agricultural farmer's bags'</u> and fell to the ground.

A. no change

B. agricultural farmers' bags

C. agricultural farmer's bags

D. agricultural farmers' bags

C is the correct answer. We are talking about a singular farmer, and so the rule for possessives is simple: add an apostrophe "s" to the end of the noun, and we're good to go!

6) Despite <u>its' usefulness</u>, irrigation did not immediately spread everywhere.

A. no change

B. its usefulness

C. its' usefulness

D. it usefulness

B is the correct answer. As mentioned previously, the word "it" can often be tricky, and it is easiest just to remember that unless you mean to say "it is," "its" never needs an apostrophe.

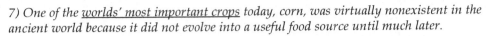

7) One of the <u>worlds' most important crops</u> today, corn, was virtually nonexistent in the ancient world because it did not evolve into a useful food source until much later.

    A. no change

    B. worlds most important crops

    C. world's most important crops

    D. most important crops' in the world

We are not talking about multiple worlds in this sentence — it's not quantum physics — so the original construction (and therefore answer A) is incorrect. Instead, we need to look at the singular noun and simply add an apostrophe "s." Thus, C is the correct answer.

Longer Passage Practice

The Great Depression

For many countries in the world, the 1920s were a time of economic prosperity and celebration. In each country, the <u>banking systems's loan policies [1]</u> made it easier for regular people to borrow money and purchase whatever they desired. As a result, people hosted large and raucous parties, even despite the <u>18th Amendments' prohibition [2]</u> on the sale of alcohol. Movies became increasingly popular, drawing thousands of people to theaters everyday. By the end of the decade, "talkies" meant that for the first time, audience members could actually hear <u>the actors' voices [3]</u>. Baseball was quickly becoming the national sport in America. People were enjoying themselves, and many believed the good times would last forever. They were wrong.

The crash of <u>Wall Streets' stock market [4]</u> in 1929 brought upon perhaps the worst economic downturn in world history. Almost overnight, the world went from celebrating seemingly never-ending amounts of wealth to panicking about bankruptcy. <u>Investors' watched [5]</u> much of the money they had invested in stocks and bonds disappear, while people who simply left their money in the bank suffered heavy losses.

1. **A.** NO CHANGE
    B. banking systems' loan policies
    C. banking systems loan policies
    D. banking system's loan policies

2. **A.** NO CHANGE
    B. the 18th Amendments's prohibition
    C. the 18th Amendment's prohibition
    D. the 18th Amendment' prohibition

3. **A.** NO CHANGE
    B. the actor's voices
    C. the voices's of the actors
    D. the voices' of the actors

4. **A.** NO CHANGE
   B. Wall Street stock market
   C. Wall Street's stock market
   D. stock market, Wall Street's

5. **A.** NO CHANGE
   B. Investors
   C. Investors'
   D. Investors's

Answers

1. D
2. C
3. A
4. C
5. B

2—Semicolons and Colons

In general, colons are used for lists; semicolons (like this one) are used to separate two complete sentences (like these).

Both types of punctuation are tested often on the SAT/ACT.

Semicolons

1) Comma Splice

Commonly referred to as *comma splice*, this rule actually refers to semicolons. However, it takes its name from the mistake many people make when they try to separate two complete sentences with a comma rather than a semicolon.

For example:

> *San Francisco is a small city with a large population, this results in a great deal of traffic congestion.*

This is really two sentences joined at the hip that need to be surgically separated, using a semicolon or employing different phrasing.

Here are two common ways to correct the problem:

(a) Use a semicolon

> *San Francisco is a small city with a large population; this results in a great deal of traffic congestion.*

(b) Subordinate one part of the sentence to the other

> *San Francisco is a small city with a large population, resulting in a great deal of traffic congestion.*

A third way is also possible: using conjunctions like *however, therefore, consequently* and *thus* preceded by a semicolon and followed by a comma. For example:

> *Napoleon marched into Russia in 1812 expecting a quick and easy victory; however, the cruel Russian winter decimated his troops and weakened French military dominance.*

In summary, when a conjunction like "however" is used BETWEEN two complete sentences, be sure to use a semicolon before the conjunction and a comma after the conjunction. Here's another, simpler, example:

We planned to go to the beach; however, the weather was bad.

The decision was made; therefore, we followed orders.

Note: A semicolon is **not** needed, for example, in the following single sentence:

The weather, however, was bad.

2) Simplify lists

When a sentence already has commas used for describing certain items, semicolons are needed to prevent confusion in the sentence. For example:

The President has small, fast boats, large, private planes, and luxury, black cars at her disposal.

In this case, you can use semicolons to enhance the clarity of the sentence:

The President has small, fast boats; large, private planes; and luxury, black cars at her disposal.

Note: Just so you know, this situation rarely occurs on the SAT/ACT. Rule number (1) is much more common.

Colons

1) Making a list, checking it twice

Colons are used to introduce lists:

When traveling, the President uses a variety of different vehicles: boats, planes, helicopters, and cars.

However, for test prep purposes, colons **cannot** be used after a verb, a preposition, or after the words *especially, as, such as,* and *including.* For example:

Wrong — Washington D.C. is: fun, exciting, and historical.

Wrong — Washington D.C. is full of: museums, federal government buildings, and restaurants.

Wrong — Washington D.C. is especially: fun, exciting, and historical.

2) Comma used as a semicolon

Colons can also be used to join two sentences together, but only when the first sentence is augmented or amplified by the second.

For example:

> *The President often flies on planes: the fleet owned by the Federal Government is particularly fast.*

Note: Think of this as a list of one. And understand that a semicolon could just as easily have been used here. Also be aware that the SAT/ACT will never give you *both* choices as possible answers to this type of question.

Practice Q&A

Working through these practice questions with follow-up explanations will help you put all of these comma rules into action. You know the drill.

1) Ever since he could walk he <u>was described as: agile</u>, strong, and above all, fast.

    A. no change

    B. he was described as — agile

    C. he was described as; agile

    D. he could be described as agile

Here, the correct answer is D. Remember that a colon cannot be placed between words like "as."

2) When times got tough, he resorted to <u>his second-best option; living</u> at home while commuting each day to San Francisco.

    A. no change

    B. his second-best option: living

    C. his second-best option living

    D. his second-best option; he was living

Option A is incorrect; you can only use a semicolon between two complete sentences. The correct answer is B. In this case, the second half of the sentence summarizes the first half, and a colon is needed between the two independent clauses to set the idea off. Option D is also incorrect because it adds unnecessary wordiness to the sentence without providing any additional clarity.

3) Despite Jackie Robinson's talent, he had one major <u>hurdle to overcome: professional baseball's</u> color barrier.

    A. no change

    B. hurdle to overcome professional baseballs'

    C. hurdle to overcome, professional baseballs'

    D. hurdle to overcome (professional baseballs')

The correct answer is A, no change. The colon is needed to set off the rest of the sentence. Use the same rule as you did above, remembering that when the second half of the sentence summarizes the first half, a colon is needed in between to introduce the following important idea.

4) When he arrived at practice, he was greeted by <u>angry teammates armed with: cruel words and even crueler intentions</u>.

   A. no change
   B. angry teammates armed with cruel words and even crueler intentions
   C. angry teammates armed with – cruel words and even crueler intentions
   D. angry teammates armed with (cruel words) and even crueler intentions

The correct answer is B. Colons are not necessary between words like "with" and the objects that follow, and the sentence flows easily and with clarity without any added emphasis from dashes or from parentheses.

5) Ancient Greek philosophy is a subject commonly studied in schools <u>today, it demonstrates</u> fundamental principles that many people tend to take for granted.

   A. no change
   B. today: it demonstrates
   C. today; they demonstrate
   D. today, yet it demonstrates

B is the correct answer here, because the second half of the sentence is an independent clause that needs something more substantial than the comma in place at present. There is no contradiction between the two ideas, so "yet" is not needed either (answer D).

6) The little that scholars know about Socrates's life comes from the writings of Plato, Xenophon, and <u>Aristophanes: no public records</u> of Socrates's life have survived.

   A. no change
   B. Aristophanes, yet no public records
   C. Aristophanes, and no public records
   D. Aristophanes because no public records

The correct answer is D. A colon is not the correct grammatical addition because the second half of the sentence does not augment the first. At the same time, the public records are not contradictory to the introductory information in the first phrase, so B is not correct. Since the public records explain why scholars know little about Socrates's life, D is the correct choice.

Longer Passage Practice

The Building of Central Park

By the middle of the 19th century, New York City was facing a growing problem: its population [1] had quadrupled since 1821 and its residents had few open spaces where they could unwind. Many cultural commentators at the time called for a great public park in the middle of Manhattan. Others called for something larger; they wanted [2] a system of parks throughout the city. After many years of difficult negotiation and sometimes uncomfortable city council meetings, the city and the park proponents reached a compromise in 1857: they would [3] open a large park in Manhattan and call it Central Park.

The Central Park Commission: the body charged with overseeing the development of Central Park, held [4] a design contest to see who could design the best park. The winning design, entitled the Greenswald Plan, was Calvert Vaux and Frederick Law Olmsted's. The two men emphasized the kind of naturalistic, open spaces common to many parks of New England, the main [5] difference here was that this park needed to account for the largest urban population in America. Because of this massive scale, Olmsted and Vaux came up with a brilliant innovation, they would [6] build separate passageways for pedestrians, cyclists, and "pleasure vehicles," which would allow each group to travel through the park without impeding another.

1. **A.** NO CHANGE
   B. growing problem: its population
   C. growing problem: its' population
   D. growing problem, it's population

2. **A.** NO CHANGE
   B. larger, they wanted
   C. larger, they wanted:
   D. larger: they wanted

3. **A.** NO CHANGE
   B. in 1857 they would
   C. in, 1857, they would
   D. in 1857, they would

4. **A.** NO CHANGE
   B. Commission, the body charged with overseeing the development of Central Park, held
   C. Commission the body charged with overseeing the development of Central Park, held
   D. Commission, the body charged with: overseeing the development of Central Park held

5. **A.** NO CHANGE
   B. New England. The main
   C. New England, the main:
   D. New England the main

6. **A.** NO CHANGE
   B. innovation they would
   C. innovation, they would,
   D. innovation: they would

Answers

1. B
2. D
3. A
4. B
5. B
6. D

3—Commas and Dashes

Most of us learned how to use commas briefly in elementary school and, since that halcyon time, have let the details slip about their exact use in practice. Lot of cultural confusion as well. Here's a quick refresher on commas and their significant other, dashes.

Commas

1) Separating three or more things in a series

For example:

> *He jumped into the water, swam a couple laps, and hopped out.*

Use a comma (called a Harvard or Oxford comma) between all the items in the series. Here's another, simpler example:

> *I like to run, fish, and swim.*

Note: The Harvard comma is only mandatory in SAT/ACT English. Many writers skip the final comma before the *and* as an unnecessary and unwanted intrusion. That's OK for them as long as they're consistent in usage.

However no comma is needed when separating compound predicates or nouns in a sentence.

For example:

> *I like to fish and swim.*
>
> *The book was both interesting and well-written.*
>
> *The apple and the avocado are both fruits.*

2) Connecting sentences with small conjunctions

FANBOYS (*for, and, nor, but, or, yet, and so*) must be preceded by a comma when connecting two independent sentences. For example:

> *He jumped into the water, but soon hopped out because of its freezing temperature.*

Note: As noted in the previous chapter, when using more elaborate conjunctions like *however, consequently, therefore,* and *thus* between two independent sentences, you must use a semicolon, **not** a comma. AND, you must use a comma after the conjunction, like this:

William Gaddis is a great American author; however, his work is seldom appreciated and rarely read.

3) Subordinating details

In order to prevent confusion when reading, we use commas after introductory phrases (exactly like this sentence itself). For example:

Jumping into the water, he suddenly felt the icy pain of the unheated pool.

There are some notable exceptions to this rule. When a sentence ends with a "because" clause, it does not ALWAYS need to be set off with a comma. For example:

The young man quickly hopped out of the water because it was so cold.

Here, a comma after "water" would only slow the reading of the sentence without providing any additional clarity.

On the other hand, sometimes phrases with "because" do need to be separated out with a comma: this occurs when the introductory phrase is indeed independent from the rest of the sentence. For example:

I knew the young man would jump out of the water, because I remembered that the pool was always unheated in the summer.

The comma is necessary here since the young man is not jumping out of the water *because* I know the pool is unheated. The clause needs to be separated to make the meaning clear.

And finally, when using "because" to start a sentence, it's best to set the phrase off with commas. For example:

Because the water was freezing, we decided to stay out of the pool.

4) Inserting parenthetical elements

A parenthetical element is a part of the sentence that could be removed without changing the meaning of the sentence; it's simply extra information. Use a comma to separate out, for clarity, this extraneous information from the rest of the sentence:

The young man, often afraid of unexpected experiences, jumped into the water.

More technically, an appositive is the name used for a parenthetical element that must be set off with commas. Think of it as a u-haul trailer attached to the main truck of the sentence.

The young man left the party broken-hearted, a shell of his former self

5) Quoting others

Use a comma between the part of the sentence that introduces the quoted passage and the quote itself. For example:

Forrest Gump once said, "Life is like a box of chocolates."

However, if the quote is introduced by the word "that" or is part of a larger structure, do not use a comma:

Forrest Gump said that "life is like a box of chocolates."

Note: Notice that the concluding quotes in both cases come **after** the period, **not before**.

6) Comma Splice

We saw this rule in the last chapter; however, it bears repeating here, since it's a popular inclusion in SAT/ACT test questions.

For example:

San Francisco is a small city with a large population, this results in a great deal of traffic congestion.

This is really two sentences joined at the hip that need to be surgically separated, using a semicolon or employing different phrasing. A simple comma won't do it.

Here are three common ways to correct the problem:

(a) Use a semicolon

San Francisco is a small city with a large population; this results in a great deal of traffic congestion.

(b) Subordinate one part of the sentence to the other

San Francisco is a small city with a large population, resulting in a great deal of traffic congestion.

(c) Use a period to separate the sentences

San Francisco is a small city with a large population. This results in a great deal of traffic congestion.

Dashes

On ACT/SAT grammar questions, dashes are often interchangeable with commas.

1) Introducing emphasized material

Dashes indicate that the words between them are important and worth paying attention to, and can be used to introduce or conclude important ideas.

> *Forrest Gump was full of folksy wisdom – life is indeed like a box of chocolates – and personal charm.*

Alternatively, dashes can be used to set off phrases that provide additional information:

> *Summer in Boston – hot, humid, and a little overcrowded – was not my cup of tea.*

Finally, dashes can be used to set off appositives at the end of a sentence:

> *The Hindenburg was inflated with hydrogen gas – a highly volatile substance.*

All the dashes in the sentences above can be replaced with commas.

2) Interchangeable with commas

To further emphasize the point, both of the following sentence pairs are correct. and interchangeable.

(a) *Caesar quietly crossed the Rubicon — an event of historic proportions.*
Caesar quietly crossed the Rubicon, an event of historic proportions.

(b) *Houdini — a man of many talents — astonished the world with his magic tricks.*
Houdini, a man of many talents, astonished the world with his magic tricks.

3) NOT Interchangeable with commas

When a subordinate clause or phrase (sentence fragment) is used to *introduce* a sentence, a comma must be used, never a dash. For example:

> **good:** *Arriving early, the speaker reviewed his notes.*

> **bad:** *Arriving early — the speaker reviewed his notes.*

> **good:** *In the year 2000, computer systems were expected to crash.*

> **bad:** *In the year 2000 — computer systems were expected to crash.*

Finally, a dash can't replace a comma in structures like this:

> **good:** *The weather was bad; however, we preservered.*

> **bad:** *The weather was bad; however — we preservered.*

Practice Q&A

Working through these practice questions with follow-up explanations will help you put all of these comma rules into action. Don't skimp.

1) College can be exciting, educational, fun, <u>and, stressful – all at the same time.</u>

   A. no change
   B. and stressful – all at the same time.
   C. and stressful, all, at the same time.
   D. and, stressful, all at the same time.

The correct answer is B, because in this sentence the commas are used to set off a list. The "and" conjunction is part of the final adjective of the list, "stressful," and therefore does not need to be separated from the rest of the sentence. An easy way to tackle this type of question is to read it "out loud" (or at least, as much as possible in an exam room) to see what flows most easily in regular English conversation.

2) Some professors assign hundreds of pages of <u>reading each week which can be</u> overwhelming if not tackled properly.

   A. no change
   B. reading, each week, which can be
   C. reading each week, which, can be
   D. reading each week, which can be

This question refers to the grammar rule introduced above about parenthetical, introductory clauses. Here, a comma is needed between the first half of the sentence, introducing the idea that professors assign a lot of reading in college, to the second half of the sentence, which talks about the personal consequences of falling behind. Thus, the correct answer is D.

3) The University of Michigan boasts <u>huge levels of school pride, but</u> the winters are particularly cold and long.

   A. no change
   B. huge levels of school pride but
   C. huge levels, of school pride, but
   D. huge, levels of school pride but

The correct answer is A. Remember that when connecting independent clauses, a comma is needed between the two clauses for clarity in reading.

Copyright © 2016

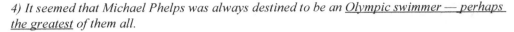

4) It seemed that Michael Phelps was always destined to be an <u>Olympic swimmer — perhaps the greatest</u> of them all.

    A. no change
    B. Olympic swimmer: perhaps the greatest
    C. Olympic swimmer perhaps the greatest
    D. Olympic swimmer; perhaps the greatest

The correct answer is A. Here, both a semicolon and a colon are grammatically incorrect because the second half of the sentence is not an independent clause and could not exist on its own. At the same time, the idea introduced in the second half of the sentence is important information that could be set off with a dash, so the original sentence is correct.

Note: The SAT/ACT will never require you to choose between a comma and a dash since the two are technically interchangeable. The following sentence would also be correct: *It seemed that Michael Phelps was always destined to be an <u>Olympic swimmer, perhaps the greatest</u> of them all.*

5) One <u>man – famous across the land, was</u> ready for the challenge.

    A. no change
    B. man: famous across the land was
    C. man famous across the land, was
    D. man — famous across the land — was

The correct answer is D. This is because the added detail "famous across the land" is important for the understanding of the sentence, and the dashes create an emphasis on the detail in a grammatically correct way. Choice A is wrong since you can never use a dash AND a comma. Choose either **two** dashes or **two** commas to set off the extra information.

6) *New York University located in the heart of Manhattan has access to theaters, restaurants, and other cultural institutions*.

    A. no change

    B. New York University, located in the heart of Manhattan, has access to theaters, restaurants, and other, cultural institutions.

    C. New York University, located in the heart of Manhattan, has access to theaters, restaurants, and other cultural institutions.

    D. New York University located in the heart of Manhattan has access to theaters, restaurants, and other, cultural institutions.

Here, we have to focus on multiple elements of comma usage to pick the correct sentence. The extra information about the location of NYU must be set off with a comma because it is an appositive. But we also need to look at the list in the second half of the sentence, taking care to choose the sentence that reads, "theaters, restaurants, and other cultural institutions" according to our first comma usage rule. The correct answer is C.

7) *I went to North Africa and then flew to Turkey*.

    A. no change

    B. and, then flew to turkey.

    C. and then, flew to Turkey.

    D. and then flew, to Turkey.

This sentence can be tricky because it may initially appear to require a comma – there are two clauses, one about traveling to Africa and the other about traveling to Turkey. However, there is no subject for the second clause; consequently, the sentence does not require a comma. The correct answer is A.

8) *During his summers, he likes to read books about happiness wisdom and science*.

    A. no change

    B. happiness, wisdom, and, science.

    C. happiness, wisdom and, science.

    D. happiness, wisdom, and science.

The correct answer is D. To answer this question, refer back to the first comma usage grammar rule, and remember that commas in lists must be used between every item in the series, in this case happiness, wisdom, and science.

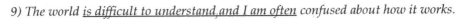

9) *The world is difficult to understand, and I am often confused about how it works.*

    A. no change
    B. is difficult to understand, and I am often
    C. is difficult to understand, and, I am often
    D. is difficult to understand and I am, often

The correct answer is B. Here, the "and" sets off two independent clauses. Independent clauses are sentences that could stand on their own as simple sentences, and this is the case with the two ideas introduced here. Thus, they must be connected with a comma. FANBOY rule.

Longer Passage Practice

Travelling in Berlin

A few months ago, I got caught in a spring hailstorm while out and about in Kreuzberg, a trendy neighborhood in Berlin. My intention was to <u>pass some time, and wait it out, [1]</u> but the hail was steadily increasing in size. Against my better judgment I sought refuge in an ominous-looking building, complete with <u>gargoyles, spires, and turrets [2]</u>. Happily, however, my safe haven had much more to offer than <u>a roof, safety, from the angry ice storm, and the bitter ghosts of past inhabitants [3]</u>.

Based on my exploration that day, I am convinced that somewhere in <u>this amazing, building, [4]</u> lies true magic. Where else could I find a place that offers free contemporary art exhibitions, a mime school, open-air cinema, <u>an international forum, for the science of dance, [5]</u> extensive studio space, and a home for countless other interdisciplinary art projects? Furthermore, how many of those buildings are <u>former hospitals, and nursing institutes [6]</u> that were once occupied by a group of artistic squatters?

This building, called the Kunstquartier Bethanien, boasts hallways like <u>the panels of a comic strip and courtyards [7]</u> that offer secret gardens and deteriorating art projects. The complex served as a hospital until 1970, when it was slated for demolition. Luckily, civilian protesters managed to convince the city to keep the space for <u>social, and cultural, [8]</u> purposes. The former nurses' quarters, however, have a more controversial history. Occupied by artists starting in 1971, the Georg-von-Rauch-Haus (as it was called by its inhabitants) was a group whose members organized a youth center and formed a voice on the local political stage. With its doctrine of <u>community, and decision-making, [9]</u> squatting was both a lifestyle choice and political statement. Despite several raids, the house is still in use as a place for collective living.

1. **A.** NO CHANGE
   B. pass some time and wait it out,
   C. pass some time and wait it out
   D. pass, some time, and wait it out

2. **A.** NO CHANGE
   B. gargoyles spires and turrets.
   C. gargoyles spires, and turrets.

    D. gargoyles, spires, and turrets,

3. **A.** NO CHANGE
    B. a roof, safety, from the angry ice storm and the bitter ghosts of past inhabitants
    C. a roof, safety from the angry ice storm, and the bitter ghosts of past inhabitants
    D. a roof, safety, from the angry ice storm, and the bitter ghosts, of past inhabitants

4. **A.** NO CHANGE
    B. this, amazing building
    C. this, amazing building,
    D. this amazing building

5. **A.** NO CHANGE
    B. an international forum, for the science, of dance
    C. an international forum for the science, of dance,
    D. an international forum for the science of dance,

6. **A.** NO CHANGE
    B. former hospitals, and, nursing institutes
    C. former hospitals, and nursing institutes,
    D. former hospitals and nursing institutes

7. **A.** NO CHANGE
    B. the panels, of a comic strip, and courtyards
    C. the panels of a comic strip, and courtyards,
    D. the panels of a comic, strip and courtyards

8. **A.** NO CHANGE
    B. social, and, cultural
    C. social and cultural
    D. social and cultural,

9. **A.** NO CHANGE
    B. community, and, decision-making
    C. community and decision-making
    D. community and decision-making,

Answers

1. B
2. A
3. C
4. D
5. D
6. D
7. A
8. C
9. D

Punctuation Cheat Sheet

Here, in a nutshell, are the most common punctuation mistakes on the SAT/ACT grammar sections (called, respectively, the Writing and English sections.) For ease in spotting the mistakes and corrections, I've included a stripped down version of each sentence using **SVO** (subject, verb, object) as a shorthand substitute.

wrong — *The world is full of princes and paupers, this results is an uneven distribution of wealth.*
reason: You can't connect two complete sentences with a comma.
SVO, SVO.

correct — The world is full of princes and paupers; this results is an uneven distribution of wealth.
reason: A semicolon is used to separate two complete sentences.
SVO;SVO

correct — *The world is full of princes and paupers: this results is an uneven distribution of wealth.*
reason: A colon, while normally associated with lists, can also be used to separate two complete sentences. In this case, a colon and a semicolon are essentially interchangeable
SVO:SVO

correct — *The world is full of princes and paupers, resulting in an uneven distribution of wealth.*
reason: Instead of two complete sentences, you can use a sentence fragment (appositive) for one, prefaced by a comma.
SVO, fragment

correct — *The world is full of princes and paupers, and this results is an uneven distribution of wealth.*
reason: When small conjunctions like *and* and *but* (the so-called FANBOYS) separate two complete sentences, a comma is necessary.
SVO, and SVO

correct — *The world is full of princes and paupers. This results is an uneven distribution of wealth.*
reason: The most basic, but the least common, test prep correction is to use a period to end the first sentence and a capital to start the second.
SVO. SVO

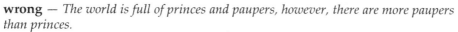

wrong — *The world is full of princes and paupers, however, there are more paupers than princes.*

reason: You can't connect two complete sentences with a comma before and after *however*.

SVO, however, SVO

correct — *The world is full of princes and paupers; however, there are more paupers than princes.*

reason: When using a transition word like *however* (technically a conjunctive adverb) between two complete sentences you must use a semicolon in front of the conjunction and a comma directly after. This rule also covers transition words like: *consequently, therefore, subsequently, otherwise, furthermore, moreover* and so on.

SVO; however, SVO

correct — *Paupers, however, are more common than princes.*

reason: When using a transition word in a single sentence, you must set the word off with commas.

S, however, VO

correct — *The world is full of diverse individuals: princes, paupers, and party-goers.*

reason: Always use the Harvard comma for every member of an SAT/ACT list.

SVO: a, b, and c

wrong — *The world is full of diverse individuals: princes, paupers and party-goers.*

reason: For test prep purposes, the Harvard comma is required for all members of a list.

SVO: a, b and c

wrong — *The little dog laughed and ate its' food.*

reason: Never use an apostrophe after *its*. The possessive form stands along. The sentence should read: *The dog ate its food.*

wrong — *The little dog laughed, and ate its food.*

reason: Never use comma with a compound verb. The sentence should read: *The dog laughed and ate its food.*

Copyright © 2016

34

4—Misplaced Modifiers

Grammar doesn't have to be boring. Sure, we could put each other to sleep talking about participial phrases and clauses. Instead, for this next rule, I'll present a stark visual for you to hold on to. Here it is:

Leaking Oil

Leaking oil, the mechanic fixed the car.

Clearly, it's the car, not the mechanic, that has the oil leak. See what I mean? When a sentence has a subordinated lead-in like this, I tell students to make sure that the first noun after the comma points back to the action being described. The sentence should read:

Leaking oil, the car was fixed by the mechanic.

Here's a second example:

As a boy, my grandma read me bedtime stories.

Is your grandma a boy? In this day and age, who knows? And, you may be thinking, who cares? Well, the SAT/ACT watchdogs care. Consequently, for clarity of exposition, remember this: the first noun after the comma has to point back to the action being described. The sentence should read:

As a boy, I was read bedtime stories by my grandma.

Practice Q&A

1) Throwing a temper tantrum, <u>the teacher</u> reprimanded the four-year-old.

    A. no change
    B. the teacher has repeatedly reprimanded the four-year-old.
    C. the four-year-old was reprimanded by the teacher.
    D. the four-year-old reprimanding the teacher.

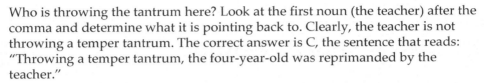

Who is throwing the tantrum here? Look at the first noun (the teacher) after the comma and determine what it is pointing back to. Clearly, the teacher is not throwing a temper tantrum. The correct answer is C, the sentence that reads: "Throwing a temper tantrum, the four-year-old was reprimanded by the teacher."

2) World-renowned for his stand-up comedy ability, <u>Jon Stewart's final closing speech</u> received over three million views on YouTube.

    A. no change

    B. the closing speech of Jon Stewart received over three million views on YouTube.

    C. the final closing speech received over three million views on YouTube.

    D. Jon Stewart received over three million views on YouTube for his final closing speech.

Use the same strategy here as you did for the last question. Is Jon Stewart world-renowned for his stand-up comedy ability, or is his speech? Although both might be true, the author most likely meant to suggest that Jon Stewart is world-renowned for his stand-up comedy ability. Therefore, the sentence must be changed to reflect that, and the answer is D: "Jon Stewart received over three million views on YouTube for his final closing speech."

3) After winning his eighth gold medal in the 2008 Olympics, <u>the records</u> of Michael Phelps were attributed to his long hours of training and natural talent.

    A. no change

    B. the long hours of training and natural talent were stated as the reason for Michael Phelps's records.

    C. Michael Phelps's records were attributed to his long hours of training and natural talent.

    D. Michael Phelps attributed his records to long hours of training and natural talent.

To spot these errors in the exam, look for the noun following the modifying phrase and check that the two work together. In this case, the records didn't win eight gold medals, Michael Phelps did, so we need to make Michael Phelps the subject of the second part of the sentence: "Michael Phelps attributed his records to long hours of training and natural talent." (Answer: D).

4) *Only Stanford University* accepted two students from our school.

   A. no change
   B. Stanford University accepted only two students from our school.
   C. From our school, only Stanford accepted two students.
   D. Stanford University accepted students from our school only.

Clearly, Stanford accepts students from more than one school so D is incorrect. C makes a similar mistake as more than one University accepts students from the school. The correct answer is B, where Stanford accepted only two students from the school. Grammar rules are also logic rules!

5) *Demolishing everything in its path, the house failed to withstand the hurricane.*

   A. no change
   B. the house failed the hurricane.
   C. the house was unable to withstand the hurricane.
   D. the hurricane destroyed the house.

What is demolishing everything in its path? Again, look at the first noun (the house) after the comma and determine what it is pointing back to. Clearly, the hurricane, not the house, is demolishing everything in its path. The correct answer is D and the sentence should read: "Demolishing everything in its path, the hurricane destroyed the house."

6) *Exhausted from two months abroad, a return flight home elicited much excitement.*

   A. no change
   B. Susie's return flight home elicited much excitement.
   C. the return flight home of Susie elicited much excitement.
   D. Susie was excited on her return flight home.

This sentence has an error that is very similar to the misplaced modifiers we've been working with in previous examples, but it's technically known as a dangling modifier, where the subject, Susie, is not even mentioned. B and C may appear to be good answers, but it is not the return flight home that is exhausted from two months abroad but Susie herself, so D is the correct choice.

Copyright © **2016**

Longer Practice Passage

Your turn. Take it away.

The Ups and Downs of a Trip to the Supermarket

For lots of people, grocery shopping is a necessary evil. Most people go to the grocery store at night after coming home from work. Already exhausted when they arrive, [1] the aisles are often crowded with other people, making the stop on the way home an exhausting one. For these reasons, it is rarely a pleasant experience for shoppers. But I like to take a different approach. Thinking of preparing my own food, [2] cooking is one of my favorite pastimes!

Arranged in colorful bins before me,[3] vegetables from all over the world present themselves. Eggplants, spinach, olives and artichokes are especially colorful. I poke and prod the items, looking for the freshest produce. Thinking of the evening meal, [4] a spinach salad with eggplant artichokes and olives sounds perfect.

1. **A.** NO CHANGE
   B. shoppers navigate the overcrowded aisles, making the stop on the way home even more tiring.
   C. the journey only makes them more tired, which is why the aisles are often crowded with other people.
   D. the aisles make stopping on the way home even more tiring.

2. **A.** NO CHANGE
   B. one of my favorite pastimes is cooking!
   C. I turn my focus to the vegetable section.
   D. enjoyable recipes occupy my time.

3. **A.** NO CHANGE
   B. my senses are bursting with the freshness of vegetables.
   C. the store is filled with vegetables, bursting with freshness at the seams.
   D. from all over the world the vegetables present themselves to me.

4. **A.** NO CHANGE
   B. perfection includes a salad of eggplant, artichokes and olives.
   C. I imagine a salad of eggplant, artichokes and olives.
   D. eggplant, artichokes and olives make a perfect salad.

Answers

1. B
2. C
3. A
4. C

5—Pronouns and Prepositions

As you can probably surmise by now, grammar is a tricky subject. Too many traps, too many potential pitfalls. It may even seem that the SAT/ACT game is rigged to lure students into making incorrect choices, setting them up to fail. This is nowhere more evident than with the vague and unnecessary pronouns that litter the grammar landscape. Take a look:

Ambiguous Pronouns

Example 1: *When Thelma and Louise went for a winter walk, she forgot to bring her umbrella.*

Example 2: *In New York, they like bagels.*

In the first example, **who** forgot her umbrella, Thelma or Louise?

And the second example, **who**, in New York, likes bagels? Jay-Z, Alvin Ailey dancers, construction workers? Use a picture word, something the reader can see, not a fuzzy indefinite pronoun.

Along the same line, avoid expressions with *too many its*.

TMI (too many its)

A corollary to the ambiguous pronoun rule is simple: always be suspicious of unnecessary *it* and *it's* used in SAT/ACT sentences. (Don't worry about the possessive form its since this is usually OK). For example:

It was so expensive that no one wanted it.

In this example, **what** was so expensive? A Tiffany bracelet? An Andy Warhol painting? Be specific. Jimmy Choo shoes!

Keep this mantra in mind: **It's NOT it.** Define your terms. Here's another example:

By the time he finished composing it, his personal life was troubled by increasing deafness.

This sentence has two pronoun flaws: **Who** composed **What**? The sentence should read:

> By the time **Beethoven** finished composing **his Fifth symphony**, his personal life was troubled by increasing deafness.

Finally, this rule also applies to adverbs like "then" or "there". To push this idea to the extreme, here are three terrible pronoun-and-adverb deranged SAT/ACT sentences:

> I did it. I did it then. I did it there.

What, when and where? Don't leave the reader guessing.

Pronouns After Prepositions

A fundamental rule that gets shredded in the vernacular but which must be carefully adhered to on the SAT/ACT grammar test is that subject pronouns (I, we, they, he, she) NEVER follow prepositions. Instead use me, us, them, him, or her.

How often have you heard people say: for you and I, between you and I, with you and I, about you and I and so on?

On the street you may get away with this faux pas but not on the SAT/ACT. The correct expression is: for you and *ME*, between you and *ME*, with you and *ME*, about you and *ME* and so on.

In general, the rule is this: subject pronouns come before the verb, object pronouns come after the verb and after prepositions. Just to be clear, here's a chart that contrasts subject, object and possessive pronouns.

Subject Pronouns	Object Pronouns	Possessive Pronouns
I	me	my, mine
you	you	your, yours
he, she, it	him, her, it	his, hers, its
we	us	our
they	them	their

> **Example 1:** *We the people proclaim **our** independence.*
>
> **Example 2:** *This report is confidential, strictly between you and **me**.*
>
> **Example 3:** *The revolutionary council distributed the articles to **them**.*
>
> **Example 4:** *Security guards walked with **him** across the compound.*

The exception to the rule involves **than,** which is an adverb, not a preposition, and requires a subject pronoun.

> **Example 1:** *Steven Hawking, the famous theoretical physicist, is smarter **than** I.*

> **Example 2:** *The French drink more red wine **than we**.*

Those two sentences sound weird, I agree, but this is a grammar test, not a street fest.

Pronoun Shifts

Another potential pronoun error occurs when an author starts a sentence with one type of pronoun and then shifts to another. One of the most common shifts (and one of the most commonly tested grammar topics on the SAT/ACT) is from third person pronouns (he/she/it/they) to second person pronouns (you/your/yours). Consider the following INCORRECT sentence:

> *In school, **we** learned that **you** can get a very bad rash when **you** mix too many skin products together.*

The author switches between "we" and "you" and therefore makes a pronoun shift error. The correct sentence reads:

> *In school, **we** learned that **we** could get a very bad rash if **we** mixed too many skin products together.*

Here's another example of pronoun shift errors in action:

> *If you regularly exercise and watch what you eat, most people can maintain a stable and healthy weight.*

CORRECT: *If you regularly exercise and watch what you eat, **you** can maintain a stable and healthy weight.*

CORRECT ALTERNATIVE: *If individuals regularly exercise and watch what they eat, they can maintain a stable and healthy weight.*

Note that in both, the pronouns remain consistent for the entirety of the sentence.

Practice Q&A

More practice, more practice, more practice.

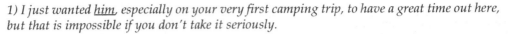

1) I just wanted <u>him</u>, especially on your very first camping trip, to have a great time out here, but that is impossible if you don't take it seriously.

    A. no change

    B. her

    C. them

    D. all of you

The correct answer is D. Notice that the pronouns in the rest of the sentence are "you" and "your," so the first pronoun needs to match with the rest. Thus, the only option that is correct is the one that uses "you," too.

2) Here at the bread factory we pride <u>themselves</u> on delivering the finest quality bread to your home.

    A. no change

    B. ourselves

    C. himself

    D. yourself

B is the correct answer. The easiest way to tackle this question may be to simply place it within the context of the sentence. Since the other pronoun is "we," the word that comes after pride must be consistent with "we." The only option that fits is therefore B, "ourselves."

3) Talking to her best girlfriend, <u>Sally found it annoying that she started texting</u>.

    A. no change

    B. Sally found her best friend annoying that she started texting.

    C. Sally found it annoying that her best friend started texting.

    D. Sally found her best friend annoying that her best friend started texting.

The correct answer is C. The question here is who lost focus – Sally or her best friend? In order to correct the sentence, we have to clarify the sentence structure, and C does this best.

Note: Remember my advice about TMI. Well, as this answer shows, sometimes you just can't avoid **it**.

4) Working as a veterinarian requires a lot of schooling and fieldwork <u>where they put academic theory into practice</u>.

    A. no change

    B. where they put their academic theory into practice.

    C. where veterinarians put their academic theory into practice.

    D. where they put veterinarian academic theory into practice.

Use the same analysis as you did above. Who is putting academic theory into practice? In this case, trained veterinarians are putting their learning to work, and so C is the correct answer.

5) Sofia and Kate walked to school everyday, except for one morning, <u>when she had an orthodontist appointment</u>.

    A. no change

    B. when Kate had an orthodontist appointment.

    C. when she had Kate's orthodontist appointment.

    D. when she went to an orthodontist appointment.

Here is another practice with the same concept as we've worked through in previous questions. Begin by asking yourself who "she" is referring to. The only sentence that clarifies this for us is B, and so this is the correct answer.

6) The conversation was private, strictly between <u>you and I</u>.

    A. no change

    B. you and me.

    C. we.

    D. you and us.

Remember that we can't use subject pronouns after prepositions like *between*. Instead, we have to use object pronouns. The correct sentence should read: "The conversation was private, strictly between you and **me**." Thus, B is the correct answer.

7) Delivering the message to <u>you and she</u> was an act of bravery.

    A. no change

    B. you and her

    C. you and us

    D. you and I

The correct answer is B. We can't use subject pronouns after prepositions like to, and so we have to use object pronouns instead. The sentence should read: "Delivering the message to you and her was an act of bravery."

Longer Passage Practice

The Story Behind Halloween

The word "Halloween" is a shortening of All Hallows' Evening, also known as Hallowe'en. If these terms sound spooky, then it is doing its job [1]: Halloween is supposed to be scary. Traditional activities include trick-or-treating, bonfires, costume parties, visiting "haunted houses" and carving jack-o-lanterns. Just between you and I[2], having participated in all of it [3] myself, I can say for certain that they are all quite entertaining. The holiday has its origins in North America starting with Irish and Scottish immigrants. After making the arduous trip to the United States, them [4] were sure to carry their most frightening traditions with them.

Halloween goes all the way back to an ancient Celtic festival known as Samhain (pronounced "sah-win"). It [5] is a celebration of the end of the harvest season in Gaelic culture. Samhain was used as a benchmark by ancient pagans; it marked the time of year when they would take stock of them [6] supplies and prepare for winter. The ancient Gaels believed that on October 31, the boundaries between the worlds of the living and the dead overlapped and the deceased would come back to life and wreak havoc. In order to avoid disaster, they had to tend to their possessions so that the dead, armed with malicious intentions, could not destroy it [7].

In traditional celebrations, bonfires are often involved. It is believed that, if burned long enough, they [8] attracted insects to the area, which in turn attracted bats to the area. Masks and costumes were worn for differing reasons: some attempted to taunt the evil spirits, while others, adopting a much more peaceful attitude, tried to appease him [9]. In modern times, trick-or-treating has become the dominant feature of Halloween. It is an activity for kids—dressed up in all manners of costume and pageantry—in which you all [10] proceed from house to house in costumes, asking for treats with the question, "Trick or treat?" The "trick" part of "trick or treat" is a threat to play a trick on the homeowner or his property if no treat is given. Homeowners beware!.

1. **A.** NO CHANGE
   B. they are doing there job
   C. they are doing their job
   D. it is doing their job

2. **A.** NO CHANGE
   B. between I and you
   C. between you and us
   D. between you and me

3. **A.** NO CHANGE
   B. them
   C. they
   D. their

4. **A.** NO CHANGE
   B. they're
   C. their
   D. the immigrants

5. **A.** NO CHANGE
   B. their
   C. there
   D. they

6. **A.** NO CHANGE
   B. there
   C. its
   D. their

7. **A.** NO CHANGE
   B. his
   C. he
   D. them

8. **A.** NO CHANGE
   B. they all
   C. them all
   D. all of them

9. **A.** NO CHANGE
   B. them
   C. your
   D. my

10. **A.** NO CHANGE
    B. they
    C. its
    D. one's

11. **A.** NO CHANGE
    B. there
    C. them
    D. their

Answers

1. C
2. D
3. B
4. D
5. A
6. D
7. D
8. A
9. B
10. B
11. D

6—Parallel Structure

One of the most important qualities of good grammar — and therefore good writing — is to keep your sentences on track, tightly focused on the message you intend to convey. If you're talking about apples, don't suddenly switch to oranges. Yeah, they're both fruit but no, they're not the same. Compare apples to apples and oranges to oranges.

This is important since it turns out that parallel structure is the single most dominant topic covered in SAT/ACT grammar. Parallel structure questions are ubiquitous and nuanced, ranging from easy to medium to hard. This section, necessarily longer and developed a little differently than the other Rules, will cover all these bases.

Verb forms should be parallel

For example:

> **bad:** *Members of the Wyoming Wilderness club like to hunt, swim and fishing.*
>
> **better:** *Members of the Wyoming Wilderness club like to hunt, swim and* **fish**.
>
> **bad:** *Most people agree that it's faster to fly than driving a car.*
>
> **better:** *Most people agree that it's faster to fly than* **to drive**.

Noun forms should be parallel

For example:

> **bad:** *Tupac Shakur was a rapper, actor and he wrote his own poetry.*
>
> **better:** *Tupac Shakur was a rapper, actor and* **poet**.

Conjunctions should be parallel

For example:

not only . . . but also

> **bad:** *The judge not only sentenced the prisoner to life he also confiscated his property.*

> **better:** *The judge **not only** sentenced the prisoner to life **but also** confiscated his property.*

Here are some other common conjunctions, demonstrated in pairs:

so . . . that

> **bad:** *The competition was of such enormous difficulty so only the most talented were able to finish.*

> **better:** *The competition was of **such** enormous difficulty **that** only the most talented were able to finish.*

neither . . . nor

> **bad:** *Neither the sports writers at the game or the athletes themselves noticed the hush that came over the stadium.*

> **better:** ***Neither** the sports writers at the game **nor** the athletes themselves noticed the hush that came over the stadium.*

either . . . or

> **bad:** *The captain of the sinking vessel was advised to either lower the lifeboats in order to avoid facing criminal charges.*

> **better:** *The captain of the sinking vessel was advised to **either** lower the lifeboats **or** face criminal charges.*

as . . . as

> **bad:** *In poker, it's often as important to play well than to play lucky.*

> **better:** *In poker, it's often **as** important to play well **as** to play lucky.*

Mistaken identity

Be careful when making comparisons. Compare apples with apples, not apples with oranges.

For example:
- **wrong** — The weather in California is better than Canada
- **correct** — The weather in California is better **than the weather** in Canada

For example:

- **wrong** — The duties of a policeman are more dangerous than a firefighter.
- **correct** — The duties of a policeman are more dangerous **than those of** a firefighter.

For example:

- **wrong** — The use of steel in construction is more prevalent than plastic.
- **correct** — The use of steel in construction is more prevalent than **the use of** plastic.

Enumerating lists

Be careful to stay parallel when enumerating lists:

bad: *Jane went to the store to buy coffee, tea, in addition to milk.*

better: *Jane went to the store to buy coffee, tea,* **and milk.**

bad: *Jane went to the store to buy coffee, tea, as well as milk.*

better: *Jane went to the store to buy coffee, tea,* **and milk.**

Shortest point exception

On the SAT/ACT, shorter sentences are usually better. However, it's sometimes necessary to add a little extra to make the sentence structure parallel.

bad: *The main reasons criminals give for ending up in jail are that they had difficult childhoods in addition to leaving school at an early age.*

better: *The main reasons criminals give for ending up in jail are that they had difficult childhoods and* **that they** *had to leave school at an early age.*

Finally, some things just go together . . .

Supply and demand, Romeo and Juliet, pizza and beer.

This is true for some noun/preposition and verb/preposition pairs, which (sorry) need to be memorized.

For example: compared with, identical to, different from (not different than!), related to, preoccupation with, capable of, need for, approve of, insist on, interest in, amused by, asserted that.

≡

Practice Q&A

You know the drill. Time to get busy.

1) Sally is not only <u>a hilarious person, but she is a kind person</u> too.

    A. no change
    B. a hilarious person but she is a kind person.
    C. a hilarious person, but she is also a kind person.
    D. a hilarious person but also a kind person.

Here, the answer is D. Remember the parallel structure rules described above of "not only," "but also" constructions. Because "a hilarious person" is an adjective and a noun, we need an adjective and a noun to follow the "but." In the original sentence, a subject and a verb follow the second half of the sentence, a hint that it is not correct. Another aspect worth noting here is that D is also the shortest answer, which is often the case for correct answers in these types of questions.

2) My favorite summer activities are <u>swimming in the pool, eating dinner out, and music</u>.

    A. no change
    B. swimming in the pool, dinner out, and listening to music.
    C. swimming in the pool, eating dinner out and listening to music.
    D. the pool, eating dinner out, and listening to music.

The trick here is to look for the pattern: since the author begins with "swimming in the pool," what follows should be a list of "doing," – eating and swimming are action verbs. By contrast, "music" is just a noun, so correct parallel structure would have "listening to music" instead. C is the correct answer because it follows this grammatical pattern.

3) Stephen Curry is admired for his <u>hard work, talent, and being an intelligent man</u>.

    A. no change
    B. hard work, talent and intelligent man.
    C. hard work, talent, and intelligence.
    D. hard work, talent and intelligence.

We want all the three words in the list to have the same construction. "Hard work" and "talent" are nouns that describe Stephen Curry, so the last word in the list should use a noun to describe him as well. The correct answer is C since "intelligence" is a noun and the structure is therefore parallel. D is incorrect since there is no comma before the "and".

4) *The everyday work of a computer scientist is more exciting than a financial analyst*.

    A. no change

    B. than people in finance.

    C. than that of a financial analyst.

    D. than finance.

The correct answer is C: "The everyday work of a computer scientist is more exciting than **that of** a financial analyst" (whether you agree with the sentiment or not!). The comparison is not appropriate here, because you can't compare work to people.

5) *Drinking sparkling water at restaurants is more exciting than tap water*.

    A. no change

    B. more exciting than drinking tap water.

    C. causes greater excitement than tap water.

    D. more exciting than that of tap water.

Use the same analysis as above, and begin by asking yourself if the comparison made here is appropriate. In this case, the act of drinking water is not comparable to tap water itself, so the sentence instead should read: "Drinking sparkling water at restaurants is more exciting than drinking tap water." The correct answer is therefore B.

6) *I like to study math, science, in addition to literature*.

    A. no change

    B. math, science, and literature.

    C. not only math and science but literature.

    D. math and science, and literature.

Here, the list of math, science, and literature need to be restructured to be parallel. The easiest way to do this is to eliminate the "in addition to," so that the sentence now reads: "I like to study math, science, and literature," and the correct answer is B.

7) *I would like to study on the East Coast because I like the weather better there in addition to living closer to my family*.

    A. no change

    B. I like the weather better there and living closer to my family.

    C. I like the weather and that of the location, living closer to my family.

    D. I like the weather better there and I like living closer to my family.

The correct answer is D, because the structure – even if it may seem repetitive to say "I like" twice in a sentence – is most parallel. Answer C is a more convoluted sentence, and B shares the same incorrect nonparallel structure as the initial sentence.

Longer Practice Passage

If You're Going to San Francisco

I have been to many cities all over the world. I have lived in New York and <u>been to visit [1]</u> Boston, Minneapolis, London, Los Angeles, Athens, Berlin, and Paris. But even though all of those cities are superb in their own ways, none of them can ever top my favorite city. Nestled on the hills west of a saltwater bay, San Francisco has so much to offer both inside and outside of the city limits. It boasts amazing opportunities for <u>education, cultural exploration, and it also has great views [2]</u> in the surrounding areas. Whether you live in San Francisco or just outside of it, it is likely that you can experience all that the Bay Area has to offer without committing yourself to hours of laborious and, as is unfortunately the case most of the time, <u>difficult travel [3]</u>.

If you love to eat, then San Francisco has you covered. The city is full of many ethnic neighborhoods that run the spectrum of cuisines. The Mission District is perhaps the most famous of such a neighborhood, noted for its delicious and, in most cases, <u>Mexican fare that is inexpensive [4]</u>. In fact, the Mission District is famous in the textbooks of food history, too: a restaurant called Taqueria La Cumbre is credited with inventing the burrito that we all know and love today. The Mission burrito combines one type of meat with tomatoes, cheese, rice, beans, sour cream, and, if you are willing to pay a premium, <u>they usually include guacamole, too [5]</u>. The district is also famous for its many festivals that, unsurprisingly, celebrate all that Mexican cuisine, <u>from its taco trucks to its hip restaurants [6]</u>, has to offer.

Another great place to spend an afternoon is Golden Gate Park, which is located on the western edge of the city and <u>is also bordering on the Pacific Ocean [7]</u>. It is somewhat similar to Central Park in New York in that it is an intricately planned, uniformly shaped, and <u>meticulously maintained public space [8]</u>. The park abounds with fun activities. My favorite is visiting the deYoung Art Museum, which houses some of the most famous paintings in the world. If you are a fan of <u>painting, drawing, and sculpturing [9]</u>, too, you could easily get lost in this place for an entire day. If you enjoy science more, however, the park is also home to the California Academy of Sciences, which is conveniently located across a grass concourse from the deYoung. Golden Gate Park's sensible design allows for people of disparate tastes to go to the park together and still have an enjoyable time!

Copyright © 2016

Venturing outside the city, you can travel northward into both <u>Napa and Sonoma County [10]</u>, which are known to grow some of the best wine grapes in the world. Both counties are home to world-famous restaurants, too, which means those with finely tuned palates and, perhaps more importantly, <u>having money to spend [11]</u> will feel right at home. The wine vineyards are situated in valleys between two moderately tall mountain ranges, so you can hike up these mountains, take in breathtaking views, and if you have the ability, <u>photographing is allowed, too [12]</u>.

1. **A.** NO CHANGE
   B. have visited
   C. visited
   D. want to visit

2. **A.** NO CHANGE
   B. education, cultural exploration, and great views, they are also available
   C. cultural exploration, education, and you can also see great views
   D. education, cultural exploration, and great views

3. **A.** NO CHANGE
   B. travel that is difficult
   C. difficulty in travel
   D. traveling difficulties

4. **A.** NO CHANGE
   B. Mexican fare, which is cheap.
   C. inexpensive Mexican fare.
   D. inexpensive things like Mexican fare.

5. **A.** NO CHANGE
   B. guacamole, too, can be added
   C. guacamole is also added
   D. guacamole

6. **A.** NO CHANGE
   B. to its taco trucks to its hip restaurants
   C. from its taco trucks from its hip restaurants
   D. from its taco trucks to, on the other hand, its hip restaurants

7. **A.** NO CHANGE
   B. the Pacific Ocean, it borders it.
   C. also borders the Pacific Ocean.
   D. is bordered on the Pacific Ocean.

8. **A.** NO CHANGE
   B. it is a public space meticulously maintained
   C. public space that is meticulously maintained.
   D. meticulously maintained, it is a public space.

9. **A.** NO CHANGE
   B. painting, drawing, and sculpture,
   C. paint, draw, and sculpture,
   D. painting, drawing, and you are interested in sculpturing,

10. **A.** NO CHANGE
    B. Napa and Sonoma Counties
    C. Counties, Napa and Sonoma,
    D. Sonoma and Napa County

11. **A.** NO CHANGE
    B. spending money is available
    C. able to spend money
    D. money to spend

12. **A.** NO CHANGE
    B. photograph what you see.
    C. photography is allowed, too.
    D. photographing, it is also allowed.

Copyright © **2016**

Answers

1. B
2. D
3. A
4. C
5. D
6. A
7. C
8. A
9. B
10. B
11. D
12. B

7—The Usual Suspects

In the real world, as opposed to the artificial world of the SAT/ACT, it's OK to use "being" in sentences that are well constructed. For example: *Being of sound mind and body, my father lived to the age of eighty.* However, on the section of the SAT/ACT where students are asked to improve the wording of a sentence, being is *ALMOST ALWAYS* the wrong choice.

Avoid Alien Beings

To drive this point home, take a look at the following sentence:

The athlete thought being strong was better than being fast.

The verb **being** doesn't supply any necessary information to the sentence. Better to remove it completely and rephrase the sentence like this:

The athlete thought strength was better than speed.

The sentence is now more straightforward and therefore more forceful. "Being" is just sentence fat that should be trimmed before serving.

Here's another example; check out the selections to see if you can trim the fat:

- **A.** Jacob has remained in political office for several terms because of being the most popular candidate.
- **B.** Being the most popular candidate, Jacob has remained in political office for several terms.
- **C.** Jacob has remained in political office for several terms, being the most popular candidate.
- **D.** Jacob, the most popular candidate, has remained in political office for several terms.

Which of these sentences is the most straightforward and direct? The correct answer is D because it gets its point across simply and directly. On the SAT/ACT grammar sections, sentences can always be improved by eliminating the word "being."

There is, There are

Another suspect grammar structure on the SAT/ACT, similar to "being," involves sentences that start with "There is" or "There are." Both are equally weak since they just unnecessarily stretch out the sentence with wishy-washy, plain-vanilla verbs. For example:

There is a great deal of controversy surrounding the ethics of stem cell research.

Much better is the shorter and simpler sentence:

A great deal of controversy surrounds the ethics of stem cell research.

Notice how "surrounds" is a much more active verb than "is."

Cutting away boring verb constructs like "There is", "There are", and "being" results in sentences that are shorter and more direct. And on the SAT/ACT, shorter is better.

Note: Back in the day, Gertrude Stein famously quipped about Oakland: "There's no there there." Good thing she didn't have to take the SAT/ACT.

Shortest Point

In American English, brevity is the heart and soul of popular expression. Think Ernest Hemingway rather than William Faulkner. Short, cryptic slogans like "Just do it" and "No pain — no gain" are part of the cultural landscape because of the direct way they convey information.

This principle holds true for SAT/ACT grammar. The most direct form of expression is the best form of expression. Take a look at the following sentences and determine which one says the most with the fewest number of words:

   A. The best way to get an exact answer to the question would be to use a calculator.
   B. Using a calculator would be the best way to get an exact answer to the question.
   C. A calculator would be the best possible way to answer the question exactly.
   D. The best way to get an exact answer is to use a calculator.

Clearly, D is the most economical expression and therefore the best choice.

Who vs. Whom

A lot of people have trouble distinguishing between restrictive and non-restrictive clauses. Think of these clauses as sub-sentences within the larger sentence. But don't worry: the SAT/ACT won't test you on that distinction. What it **will** test you on, however, is the distinction between *who* and *whom*. Here's how to pinpoint when to use one over the other.

First of all, recognize that *who* is a subject pronoun and *whom* is an object pronoun. That's important. Now, stay with me: use *whom* when a secondary verb in the sentence already has a subject and use *who* when the secondary verb is missing a subject. For example:

> *The man who saw Mary is in the room.*

The main sentence is: *The man is in the room.* The sub-sentence is: *who saw Mary.*

Just focus on the sub-sentence and notice that there's no subject in front of the secondary verb *saw.* Therefore, we have to use *who* (a subject pronoun) to take the place of the missing subject.

Now let's shift gears and rewrite the sentence like this:

> *The man whom Mary saw is in the room.*

Again, the main sentence is: *The man is in the room.* But this time the sub-sentence is: *whom Mary saw.* Notice that there's now a subject — Mary — in front of the secondary verb. Therefore, we can't use *who*: instead, we have to use *whom.* You could also re-think the sub-sentence like this: Mary saw whom?

Bottom line: when the verb in the sub-sentence needs a subject use *who*; when the verb in the sub-sentence already has a subject use *whom.* Here's another example:

> *The swimmer whom Jack saw yesterday at the pool was strolling on the beach.*
>
> *The swimmer who saw Jack yesterday at the pool was strolling on the beach.*

You can also set the sub-sentence off with commas when it's not essential to the action. For example:

> *Susan, who loves dogs, volunteers at the local SPCA.*
>
> *Susan, whom dogs love, volunteers at the local SPCA.*

Finally, just so you know, you can use *that* in place of *who* **and** *whom*:

> *The man that saw Mary is in the room.*
>
> *The man that Mary saw is in the room.*

And finally, an easy rule: after *to* or *for*, always use *whom*.

To whom it may concern . . .

For whom the bell tolls . . .

Practice Q&A

1) <u>*Being blown away by the talent of the musicians*</u>*, the crowd went crazy.*

    A. no change

    B. Blown away by the talent of the musicians

    C. Having been blown away by the talent of the musicians

    D. Blown away through the talent of the musicians

The correct answer is B. Since we are trying to avoid alien beings, think about making the sentence more direct and less wordy. The easiest way to accomplish this task is simply by eliminating "being" from the sentence.

2) *The bus driver*<u>*, being tired and homesick*</u>*, failed to abide by the traffic rules.*

    A. no change

    B. being full of tired homesickness

    C. tired and homesick

    D. having been tired and homesick

Again, think about trying to avoid alien beings. The least wordy and most direct answer is C, and thus, this is the correct answer.

3) *The bystander* <u>*who witnessed*</u> *the robbery was giving a statement to the police.*

    A. no change

    B. whom witnessed

    C. to whom was witnessing

    D. who was a witness about

Since there's no subject in front of the verb *witnessed* in the sub-sentence, you must use *who*, a subject pronoun. The correct answer is A.

4) *Failing to place at the tournament yet* <u>*again was when he decided to quit swimming*</u>*.*

    A. no change

    B. again, he decided to quit swimming.

    C. again was the moment when he decided to quit swimming.

    D. was the exact time when he decided to quit swimming.

This sentence is awkwardly phrased. Too long. We want to think about making it more direct so the shortest point rule holds here. Thus, B is the best answer.

5) It was important, the coach explained, for his players to understand that it would take hard work and effort to be successful on the football field.

 A. no change
 B. The coach explained that it was most important for his players to understand that it would take hard work and effort to be successful on the football field.
 C. The coach explained that hard work and effort were important for success on the football field.
 D. On the football field, in order to be successful, it was most important the coach explained for his players to understand that it would take hard work and effort.

The correct answer is C. Again, we are thinking about how to make the sentence shorter and more direct. The answer that accomplishes this best is obviously the one that takes up the least amount of space!

6) There are many poor people that are scrambling to make a living today.

 A. no change
 B. There are, today, many poor people scrambling to make a living.
 C. Many poor people scramble to make a living today.
 D. There are many poor people who must scramble to make a living today.

The correct answer is C. Short and sweet.

Longer Passage Practice

Family Tradition in Modern Times

The <u>Streits being the descendants of a long line of lower Manhattan business owners, [1]</u> wanted a slogan that would sum up what their business means to them and to their fellow patrons. They wanted <u>something, being genuine and representative, [2]</u> of what they were doing at Streit's. They were not just feeding hungry Jewish mouths during Passover. No, they were maintaining an Old World tradition, running a business that ran in their blood. To do this they needed a manager <u>whom</u> [3] had sufficient marketing savy to blend old with new management styles. Sam Adleson, [4] <u>who ran the company</u> for many years, had just retired. <u>There was a need and requirement for new management to fill the gap.</u> [5]

1. **A.** NO CHANGE
   B. Streits, the descendants of a long line of lower Manhattan business owners,
   C. Streits the descendants, of a long line of lower Manhattan business owners,
   D. Streits, the descendants, of a long line, of lower Manhattan business owners,

2. **A.** NO CHANGE
   B. something genuine, and representative
   C. something genuine and representative
   D. something, genuine, and representative,

3. **A.** NO CHANGE
   B. to whom
   C. who,
   D. who

4. **A.** NO CHANGE
    B. whom the company had run,
    C. for whom the company had run
    D. that had run the company

5. **A.** NO CHANGE
    B. There was a gap to be filled by new management.
    C. There was needed and required new management to fill the gap.
    D. New management was needed to fill the gap.

Answers

1. B
2. C
3. D
4. A
5. D

8—Verb Tenses

Verb tenses are at once simple, in the sense that most of us have practice with using the correct tense in everyday conversation, and complex, in that after learning the tenses in elementary school we haven't looked back. Hence this section is somewhat remedial. Move through it quickly.

> *Simple present:* They love
>
> *Present Perfect:* They have loved — *use present perfect to connect unfinished actions that happened in the past that are still occurring in the present*
>
> *Simple past:* They loved
>
> *Past perfect:* They had loved — *use past perfect to establish a sequence of events that occurred prior to other events in the past. This is not often tested on the SAT/ACT.*
>
> *Future:* They will love
>
> *Future Perfect:* They will have loved

The important thing to understand in context of the ACT/SAT is how to keep the tenses constant throughout the entire sentence. If the sentence takes place in the past, every verb must be past tense as well. Recognizing and correcting for consistency is far more crucial than memorizing the specific "types" of verbs that can be used.

Practice Q&A

The Battle of Waterloo <u>takes place</u> near Waterloo, Belgium on June 18, 1815.

- **A.** no change
- **B.** took place
- **C.** has taken place
- **D.** will have taken place

The correct answer is B. The Battle of Waterloo clearly occurred in the past, and so we need to choose an answer that reflects this idea. In context, the rest of the paragraph can help show you what the verb tense should be – remember that we are looking for consistency in our tenses. Another clue to help guide you to the answer is recognizing that B is also a much shorter answer than the alternatives, a hint that this one is the best option.

Though he was a great general, his forces were no match for the combined might of the opposing army, leaded by the Duke of Wellington.

    A. no change

    B. led

    C. were led

    D. had been lead

Utilize the "shortest point" rule in answering the question, and simplify the sentence to "He was leaded by the Duke of Wellington." When you shorten the sentence, the error becomes clearer, and the correct answer is B.

The battle's end has also marked the end of the first hundred days after Napoleon's return from exile.

    A. no change

    B. was also marked

    C. also marked

    D. did also marked

The correct answer is C. The easiest way to tackle this question is by reading it in context and listening for consistency in the sentence. Napoleon lived hundreds of years ago, so the correct answer cannot be in the present tense. Both "Was also" and "did also" have awkward syntax, which should hint that they are both incorrect alternatives.

Today, the battle was regarded as one of the most historically significant and influential battles of all time.

    A. no change

    B. had been regarded

    C. is regarded

    D. to regard

The introductory word "today" gives a big hint that this sentence must be in the present tense. Additionally, we are reflecting back on the past, another hint that "was regarded" is incorrect. Thus, the answer is C.

Until noon of June 18, 1815, Napoleon <u>delays the start</u> of the battle to give the ground time to dry.

    A. no change

    B. did delays the start

    C. did delayed the start

    D. delayed the start

The correct answer is D. "Delays" is in the present tense, and "did delays' is not much better. We need a verb that is in the past tense and without the unnecessary wordiness of "did," so D is the best answer here.

Longer Practice Passage

Rapanui

Easter Island is the world's most isolated inhabited island, <u>lying [1]</u> roughly halfway between Chile and Tahiti. The triangular shaped island <u>was [2]</u> made mostly of volcanic rock. Small coral formations can be found along the shoreline, but the lack of a coral reef <u>has allowed the sea to cut [3]</u> cliffs around much of the island. The coastline has many lava tubes and volcanic caves. The only sandy beaches are on the northeast coast. Upon first glance, it is difficult to say that Easter Island seems like a hospitable place.

The inhabitants of this charming and mysterious place, however, <u>saw [4]</u> things differently. Their nickname for it—Te Pito o TeHenua, or "the navel of the world"—reflects their reverence for the island. Archaeological evidence indicates that the island <u>has been discovered [5]</u> by Polynesians at about 400CE. In 1722, a Dutch explorer, Jacob Roggeveen, sighted and dropped anchor near the island. This happened to be on Easter Sunday, and the name stuck. Roggeveen's arrival is the first documented description of the people of Easter Island. As he <u>did write [6]</u> in his journal, he made contact with "three distinct groups of people: dark-skinned, red-skinned, and very pale-skinned people with red hair."

The formal Polynesian name of the island is Rapanui, which is a name given by a Tahitian visitor in the 19th century who <u>says [7]</u> that the island looked like the Tahitian island of Rapa, but bigger. The island's current Inhabitants are of Polynesian descent, but for decades anthropologists <u>had argued [8]</u> the true origins of these people, never quite reaching a consensus. What many early explorers who visited the island found was a scattered population with almost no discernible governmental structure. Because they were so unaccustomed to foreigners, the Easter Islanders were easy prey for 19th century slave traders. Slowly but surely, western influence <u>eroded [9]</u> the cultures of Easter Island over the past several centuries and up to the present.

1. **A.** NO CHANGE
   B. lies
   C. does lie
   D. and has been lying

2. **A.** NO CHANGE
    B. were
    C. is
    D. can be

3. **A.** NO CHANGE
    B. has allowed the sea cutting
    C. allows the sea to be cutting
    D. had allowed the sea to cut

4. **A.** NO CHANGE
    B. see
    C. have seen
    D. will see

5. **A.** NO CHANGE
    B. been discovered
    C. was discovered
    D. discovered

6. **A.** NO CHANGE
    B. has written
    C. wrote
    D. did wrote

7. **A.** NO CHANGE
    B. said
    C. will say
    D. has said

8. **A.** NO CHANGE
    B. has argued
    C. have argued
    D. will argue

9. **A.** NO CHANGE
    B. erodes
    C. has eroded
    D. will erode

Answers

1. A
2. C
3. A
4. B
5. C
6. C
7. B
8. C
9. C

9—Subject Verb Agreement

One of the most significant grammar rules for success in college and beyond has to do with matching singular subjects with singular verbs and plural subjects with plural verbs. The ACT and the SAT try to trick students by interposing prepositional phrases between the subject and verb, sort of like stuffing styrofoam peanuts into a Fedex gift box. To get to the gift, you have to first throw out the extraneous packaging. More succinctly: *subjects never follow prepositions.* For example:

> *The harmful effects of insulin resistance on the metabolic system is well known.*

Notice how the unnecessary prepositional phrases of *insulin resistance* and *on the metabolic system* subvert the true relationship between the subject and verb. The subject (harmful effects) is plural, so the verb (is) must also be plural. The sentence should read:

> *The harmful **effects** of insulin resistance on the metabolic system **are** well known.*

Note: For fun, watch a **short video** on this rule on my YouTube channel: www.youtube.com/tctutoring

Prepositions

Prepositions are place words. Your fourth-grade teacher probably told you to imagine a mouse in a house. The various directions the mouse takes in navigating the house are: over, under, around, through, beside, beyond, above, below, in, on and dozens more.

Still other prepositions point to relationships: of, with, by, for, to

Don't confuse these with other "tiny" words like articles (a, the, an) or FANBOY conjunctions (and, but, or, for, nor, yet, so).

Here's another example of the same principle:

> *The production of goods and services in advanced industrial economies are beginning to show signs of decline.*

Since the subject is singular (production), the verb must also be singular. The sentence should read:

> The **production** of goods and services in advanced industrial economies **is** beginning to show signs of decline.

To put this concept into play with SAT-style questions, consider the following examples and choose the best way to improve the sentence:

A. Each of the 5000 spectators are cheering wildly at the game.

B. The spectators cheering wildly at the game are among the 5000.

C. At the game, each of the 5000 spectators in attendance are cheering wildly.

D. Each of the 5000 spectators at the game is cheering wildly.

The answer is D.

To analyze this correctly, ignore the prepositional phrase in the sentence (of the 5000 spectators) and focus exclusively on the subject, which, in this case, is . . . "Each." Since "each" is singular, the verb must also be singular. This technique for parsing sentences is both extremely powerful and easy, once you get the hang of it. I have my students do practice test after practice test in order for the techniques to sink in.

Advanced Analysis

The basic rule of English sentence structure is this: *Subject Verb Object* (SVO). However, more complicated and sophisticated sentences in the SAT/ACT grammar section may have secondary subjects wrapped up, like Russian dolls, inside the main sentence. For example:

> Scientists warn that the **effect** of global warming on ocean currents have not been sufficiently studied.

In this example, "Scientists" is the *Subject,* "warn" is the primary *Verb* and "that the effect of global warning on ocean currents have not been sufficiently studied" is the extended *Object.* The extended Object in this case has a secondary subject/verb pair wrapped inside. To correctly analyze this type of sentence you have to "unwrap" the Object and remove the prepositional phrases that cloud the relationship between the secondary subject/verb pair. For example:

> Scientists warn that the effect have not been sufficiently studied.

After removing the prepositional phrases *of global warming on ocean currents*, it's clear that the secondary subject — more technically, the subject of the relative clause — is **effect** and the secondary verb should be **has**. The sentence should read:

*Scientists warn that the **effect** of global warming on ocean currents **has** not been sufficiently studied.*

One final note of SAT/ACT caution. Sometimes, SAT/ACT grammar questions invert the usual Subject Verb Object pattern, placing the Subject *after* the Verb. For example:

Beyond the Mojave Desert resides the dwindling Apache reservations.

"Beyond" is a preposition and subjects never follow prepositions. Therefore the subject of the sentence is **reservations** and the verb must be plural. The sentence should read:

*Beyond the Mojave Desert **reside** the dwindling Apache **reservations**.*

Practice Q&A

Drill time. More practice, more practice, more practice.

1) A few more steps – together with a quick glance around to make sure the coast is clear – <u>brings us</u> to the gate.

- **A.** no change
- **B.** bring us
- **C.** brought us
- **D.** brung us

The key here is to cut out the phrase in between the dashes, and focus on the connection between "steps" and "brings." When we simplify the sentence, we can see that steps are plural, so the verb should be "bring," and the answer is B.

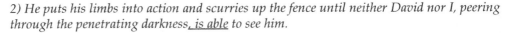

2) *He puts his limbs into action and scurries up the fence until neither David nor I, peering through the penetrating darkness, is able to see him.*

    A. no change

    B. able

    C. are able

    D. am able

This question is tricky because of the "neither" "nor" construction, but the correct answer is D, "am able." This is because "I" comes right before the clarifying phrase "peering through the penetrating darkness," so that the shortened phrase should be "I am able," versus "I are able" or "I is able," as the other answers suggest. Thus, the correct answer is D.

3) *I love caterpillars. Each and every one, some of which have spots, others which have stripes, are unique in their own way.*

    A. no change

    B. have the ability to be unique

    C. is unique

    D. appear to be unique

Begin by eliminating the distracting phrases that describe the caterpillars – when looking at the grammatical construction, details like which caterpillars have stripes and which have spots are not necessary. Now we have a sentence that reads: "each and every one are unique in their own way." We can cut the sentence down further to be "each one are unique in their own way," and now it should be clear that the correct phrasing should be that "each one is" unique, and the answer is C.

4) *When the fireflies - who typically return to their resting places very late at night - are gone away, I like to stare at the open night sky.*

    A. no change

    B. have gone away

    C. done going away

    D. leave away

This one should be fairly simple, but the key for catching the error is again, eliminating any unnecessary phrases, and then reading the sentence aloud in your head. The correct answer is B.

5) The effects of eating too much chocolate on my sleep <u>is seen</u> on Halloween and other holiday nights.

    A. no change

    B. was seen

    C. appears to be seen

    D. are seen

Remember that subjects never follow prepositions "like," "of," and "on." So, we should remove the prepositional phrase "of eating too much chocolate" and "on my sleep." Since the subject is effects, the verb must be plural. The correct answer is D.

6) Each of the days of winter on the East Coast this past year <u>were hard</u> to enjoy.

    A. no change

    B. was hard

    C. appear to have been hard

    D. are hard

By now, the pattern of approach should be quite clear. Tackle this question by removing the preposition phrase "of the days of winter on the East Coast" and the unnecessary detail "this past year," and the sentence becomes much less tricky. Because "each" is singular, the verb should be singular as well, and the correct answer is B.

7) The news reports about the future of the Greek currency <u>demonstrates the uncertainty</u> about the country's economic situation.

    A. no change

    B. demonstrate the uncertainty

    C. is a demonstration

    D. is demonstrating

The subject of the sentence is the news reports. Therefore the verb must be plural. The other noun follows a preposition and can't be the subject, so the correct answer is B: "The news reports about the future of the Greek currency demonstrate the uncertainty about the country's economic situation.

Longer Passage Practice

Charles Beeker for Governor

Because of his creative proposals for solving the state's problems and his middle-of-the-road approach, <u>Beeker is [1]</u> best suited to become Massachusetts's next governor.

On Tuesday, Massachusetts voters from different parts all over the state <u>is choosing [2]</u> their first new governor in eight years. That new governor will face a slew of substantial problems: income inequality in Massachusetts is the 8th highest in the nation, the projected decline in high school graduates <u>likely mean [3]</u> a shortage of 55,000 workers within six years, and the bureaucratic mess within government agencies like the Department of Children and Families <u>is becoming [4]</u> harder and harder to ignore. Although the economic system of the state, which suffered a serious decline in the Great Recession of 2008, <u>are growing [5]</u> and the Boston Marathon bombings ultimately brought residents closer together, Massachusetts's next governor will need creative solutions to combat these education, budget, and structural issues that are mirrored on a national scale. Charles "Charlie" Beeker is well-equipped to provide these solutions, and should be the Commonwealth's next governor.

Charlie Beeker differs from national Republicans in that he is socially liberal. He believes in the "right to choose" for abortion, agrees that climate change on a global level <u>has been a [6]</u> major issue that <u>must be addressed [7]</u> through investment in renewable energy, and supports gay marriage. He has therefore already demonstrated a willingness to align with those across the aisle. In fact, he and Democratic opponent Mary Cain have somewhat similar platforms. As the Boston Globe reports, Cain challenged the federal Defense of Marriage Act and <u>seek to protect [8]</u> women's ability to seek abortion services without harassment while serving as the state's attorney general. Where the candidates differ – education and sick time, among other issues – <u>Beeker has shine [9]</u>.

1. **A.** NO CHANGE
   B. Beeker are
   C. Beeker was
   D. Beeker will be

2. **A.** NO CHANGE
   B. were choosing
   C. appear to be choosing
   D. are choosing

3. **A.** NO CHANGE
   B. likely means
   C. appears to be likely to mean
   D. seem to mean

4. **A.** NO CHANGE
   B. have been becoming
   C. appear to be becoming
   D. are becoming

5. **A.** NO CHANGE
   B. is growing
   C. were growing
   D. was growing

6. **A.** NO CHANGE
   B. was
   C. is
   D. will be

7. **A.** NO CHANGE
   B. is addressed
   C. are addressed
   D. addresses

8. **A.** NO CHANGE
   B. seeks
   C. will be seeking
   D. sought

9. **A.** NO CHANGE
   B. Beeker has shined
   C. Beeker will be shining
   D. Beeker shines

Answers

1. A
2. D
3. B
4. A
5. B
6. C
7. A
8. D
9. D

10—Word Pairs

This section is more of a list than a set of grammar rules, but the SAT/ACT likes to test your ability to correctly match word pairs and to choose the word that fits correctly in the context of the sentence. For your review, I've listed these word pairs and some of the most frequently confused words below:

Word Pairs

1. Either . . . or

    This word pair is used in positive sentences and means "one or the other"

    The beds are always either too small or too large.

    I would be happy to eat either Indian or Italian food tonight.

2. Neither . . . nor

    This word pair is the exact converse of the last one. It is used in negative sentences and means "not this one nor the other" — in other words, neither option works.

    The bed was neither too small nor too large.

    I would be willing to eat neither Indian nor Italian food tonight.

3. Not only . . . but also

    He was not only funny and smart, but also talented on the guitar.

    I am not only tired, but also hungry.

Copyright © 2016

Frequently Confused Words

Affect vs. Effect

   A. When you affect something, you cause it to change. Affect is a verb. and it is

   B. Effect is a noun. It is a result brought about by a certain action.

     Her mood was <u>affected</u> by the weather.

     The weather had an <u>effect</u> on her mood.

And . . . Also

   A. Using these two words together is redundant.

Allusion vs. Illusion

   A. An allusion is a reference to a previous work of art, piece of music, famous play – anything that happened in the past.

   B. An illusion is a fantasy.

     Her speech was full of <u>allusions</u> to ancient Roman literature.

     The waterfall created a marvelous <u>illusion</u>.

Beside vs. Besides

   A. Beside means next to.

   B. Besides means "in addition to."

     I walk to school each day on the path <u>beside</u> the river.

     <u>Besides</u>, I never even liked him anyway.

Between vs. Among

   A. Between is a word used for two people or things

   B. Among is a word when there is more than two people or things.

     I walked <u>between</u> my mother and my sister.

     I walked <u>among</u> the crowd.

Breath vs. breathe

   A. Breath is a noun

   B. Breathe is a verb

I took a deep <u>breath</u>.

My sister <u>breathes</u> deeply when she sleeps.

Compared to vs. Compared with

A. When you are *compared to* someone, you are speaking about similarities.

B. *Compared with* can mean comparing similarities or differences.

Different than vs. Different from

A. The two phrases mean the same thing, but *different from* is more grammatically correct.

That vs. Which vs. Who

A. *That* provides necessary information needed to identify a specific thing.

B. *Which* and *who* simply add additional information

The seats <u>that</u> Mary bought on the high-speed train could not be returned.

Mary bought tickets on the high-speed train, <u>which</u> were quite inexpensive.

The man <u>who</u> I saw is in the room.

Note: Use *which* with things; use *who* with people. Use *that* with either.

Their vs. They're

A. *Their* is a possessive form, while *they're* means "they are."

<u>*Their*</u> *cars were very nice.*

<u>*They're*</u> *a bunch of really nice guys.*

Note: Who's/whose is another frequently confused set of words that follow the same rule. *Who's* is a contraction, *whose* is a possessive form of "who."

Toward vs. Towards

A. The exhausted runner limped slowly *toward* the finish line.

B. *Towards* does not exist in English. Shorter is better, even one letter.

Practice Q&A

1) *Frederick Douglass was born a slave, privileged with neither the rights <u>or the future prospects</u> of free men.*

    A. no change

    B. nor the future prospects

    C. either the future prospects

    D. and the future prospects

The correct answer is B. Remember the word pair *neither . . . nor*. This sentence simply follows that construction.

2) *Not only was Jerry responsible for household chores<u>, and he also</u> walked to school each day.*

    A. no change

    B. then he also

    C. also

    D. but he also

The correct answer is D. This is another word pair you'll just need to memorize: *not only* always goes with *but also*.

3) *By the time he was just ten years old, he could play songs on the piano <u>as well like</u> any fully-trained musician.*

    A. no change

    B. as good like

    C. as good as

    D. as well as

The correct answer is D. Always be on the lookout for the *as . . . as* grammatical construct. Twin towers of parallel structure. Also look for *so . . . as*.

4) *She was told to either love him <u>or</u> leave him.*

    A. no change

    B. and

    C. but

    D. then

The correct answer is A, no change. *Either* is a word pair that is often matched with *or*.

5) She was <u>*affected by*</u> *her older sister's actions.*

    A. no change

    B. effected by

    C. effect by

    D. affect by

The correct answer is A, no change. Remember that "affected" is a verb, while "effected" is a noun. In this sentence, we need the verb form, so the original sentence is correct.

6) *Just as cats always land on their feet,* <u>*and too does*</u> *Tommy.*

    A. no change

    B. because also

    C. then

    D. so does

We are making a comparison here, so the correct answer is D.

≡

Mixed Practice – All Rules Combined

University of Cambridge through the Years

The University of Cambridge was founded in the year 1209 CE, after several scholars left Oxford University because his [1] intellectual pursuits were perceived as religiously inappropriate. The school's motto from its founding is as follows — [2] "From this place, we gain enlightenment and precious knowledge." From the start, then, the University of Cambridge viewed knowledge as something to be cherished and protected. Now, more than 800 years later, that motto is as undeniably and inarguably true like [3] it was in the 13th century.

Currently, the University is dividing [4] up into 32 colleges, many of which have been in existence for hundreds of years. Each college have its [5] own unique characteristics. For example, Pembroke College, which was founded in 1348, has a library constructed entirely of red brick, a material not used in many buildings at the time. Kings' College [6], which takes its name from its founder King Henry VI, is home to one of the most famous chapels in the world.

Ever since it's [7] opening, the University of Cambridge has been at the center of various myths and legends. The Mathematical Bridge, which was supposedly built by Sir Isaac Newton, is said to have had no screws anywhere in its frame. One enterprising student attempting to unravel the genius of Newton's design, [8] took apart the bridge and was never able to put it back together. The bridge has since been rebuilt with screws, but the legend of Newton's seemingly impossible achievement is always living [9] on.

Another of Cambridge's famous legends is actually a true story; a wooden spoon [10] used to be awarded to the student who achieved the lowest passing grade on the end-of-year mathematics exam. Prior to the early 20th century, students' scores [11] used to be ranked from highest to lowest on a publicly available form. As a result, everyone could clearly see who had won the wooden spoon. Starting in 1909, however, scores were listed alphabetically, making it more difficult to ascertain whom [12] had the lowest score.

It can plainly be seen that the University of Cambridge is a historical landmark. Its age alone makes it older than both the United States of America or [13] the light bulb combined. Having such a storied history, a rivalry has developed between Cambridge and [14] the nearby Oxford University. The two colleges constantly feud over which college has produced more historically significant thinkers. Considering the rich intellectual histories of both institutions, such a debate <u>will likely not be becoming resolved [15]</u> anytime soon.

1. **A.** NO CHANGE
    B. her
    C. theirs
    D. their

2. **A.** NO CHANGE
    B. is as follows
    C. is as follows:
    D. is as follows;

3. **A.** NO CHANGE
    B. when
    C. but also
    D. as

4. **A.** NO CHANGE
    B. is divided
    C. is in the dividing process
    D. divides

5. **A.** NO CHANGE
    B. has it's
    C. has its
    D. have it's

6. **A.** NO CHANGE
    B. King's College
    C. Kings's College
    D. Kings College'

7. **A.** NO CHANGE
    B. it is
    C. its
    D. its'

8. **A.** NO CHANGE
   B. student, attempting to unravel the genius of Newton's design,
   C. student attempting to unravel the genius of Newton's design,
   D. student, attempting to unravel the genius, of Newton's design,

9. **A.** NO CHANGE
   B. is living
   C. will always be living
   D. lives

10. **A.** NO CHANGE
    B. a true story: a wooden spoon
    C. a true story — a wooden spoon
    D. a true story a wooden spoon

11. **A.** NO CHANGE
    B. student's scores
    C. students's scores
    D. students scores

12. **A.** NO CHANGE
    B. who
    C. whose
    D. who's

13. **A.** NO CHANGE
    B. even
    C. plus
    D. and

14. **A.** NO CHANGE
    B. Cambridge has developed a rivalry with
    C. there has developed a rivalry with
    D. a rivalry has developed among Cambridge and

15. **A.** NO CHANGE
    B. will not be resolved
    C. will, being resolved, not very likely
    D. will be, becoming resolved, not

Answers

1. D
2. C
3. D
4. B
5. C
6. B
7. C
8. B
9. D
10. B
11. A
12. B
13. D
14. B
15. B

11—Writer's Goal

Some sections of the SAT/ACT focus on determining the intent, or purpose, of the author's writing. These types of questions ask what the writer is attempting to prove; the reason for the author's essay. Although this element of testing makes many students nervous, the most important thing to understand is that **everything** the SAT/ACT asks you is a matter of *facts*.

Matter of Facts

Questions are posed objectively and the answer can **always** be found in the text. If you remember that the writer's goal is NOT a matter of opinion, you're well on your way to correctly answering the question.

The easiest way to approach this question is to read the first few sentences, trying to determine the main context of the essay. You want to be able to summarize the main idea of the story. There are different things that the author could be doing:

- **Telling a story**
- **Explaining an event (summarizing something)**
- **Explaining two different points of view (author does not pick a side)**
- **Convincing you of one specific point of view**

Once you've read enough of the passage to get a sense of what it is about, you'll want to narrow down your options on the multiple choice until you find an answer where ALL PARTS of the answer can be found in the text. In general, you want to focus on these four things when reading the passage:

- **The author's purpose is usually stated in the first or second passage**
- **Sometimes there will be a transition in the passage, marked by words like** *however, on the other hand,* **or** *therefore*
- **The evidence in the following (or preceding) paragraphs should directly support the author's purpose**

Copyright © 2016

Practice Q&A

Because these questions require in-context passages, we're going to jump straight into slightly longer practice questions right away:

If you love to listen to music, then you have also probably found yourself thinking about attending a music festival at some point in your life. The allure is obvious: your favorite bands perform in an atmosphere that is both fun and easy to navigate. Chances are that you will only have to walk a few hundred feet from one concert to another. Really, what could be easier than that? On the other hand, though, there are several drawbacks: the tickets are expensive, you may not enjoy every performer's music, and, well, they can be exhausting! Here are a few tips you might be able to use to decide whether or not a music festival sounds right for you.

In this passage, the author develops her point by:

    A. Appealing directly to the reader

    B. Telling a short story

    C. Introducing two differing viewpoints

    D. Summarizing an event

Here, the correct answer is A. Begin by reading the passage. It is clear that the passage is about music festivals, but how exactly does the author introduce the topic? In this case, she uses "you" to describe the allure that "you" must be feeling – thus, by appealing directly to the reader.

The passage continues:

Once you have made your decision, it is time to decide what exactly to bring to the festival. Some festivals require attendees to stay on site throughout the duration of the festival. In this case, it would be helpful to pack your car (or a friend's car, depending on the situation) with bottles of water and non-perishable snacks. Food at festivals often cost quite a bit of money, so if you are trying to enjoy the festival on a budget, consider bringing instant meals, too. At other festivals, though, you will arrive, stay for the day, and return home at night. In these cases, you can afford to bring fresher food and drink because they will only need to last you for one day. You can replenish your stock the next morning. Make sure you know the rules of the festival you choose to attend so you can prepare accordingly!

Suppose the writer had chosen to write an essay that indicates that describes the differences between music festivals of different musical genres. Would this passage fulfill the writer's goal?

A. No, because the writer discusses music festival food.

B. No, because the writer does not focus on the actual music heard at music festivals.

C. Yes, because the writer is insistent that readers should not attend music festivals.

D. Yes, because the writer has clearly been to several music festivals.

The correct answer is B. Although A is also true, the reason that the passage does not fulfill the writer's goal is NOT because the writer discusses music festival food, it is because the writer does not focus on the actual music heard at music festivals.

Mad Men's 1960s setting offers an opportunity to explore the relationship between current self-perceptions of greater freedom and the underlying issues of loneliness present in the show and today. At first glance, main character Don Draper appears to represent what many wish to be. He breaks the rules – he smokes, he drinks, he dominates at work and at home, cheats and then pays little consequence. Don is an extreme form of an American ideal – the vaunted individualist Emerson might have glorified in "Self-Reliance" a hundred years before. Yet after one season of the show, few would want to be Don Draper. This is why Anthony Weiner's Mad Men, about the tumultuous lives of New York City advertising executives and their families, is relevant despite the changes in explicit societal rules: even as it glamorizes Don's self-reliance, it reveals how guarded, exclusionary independence can undermine influence. And even as it celebrates American individualism amidst dizzying change, it exposes the consummate consequence of an inability to rely on other people – few meaningful relationships, and debilitating isolation. It is through deeply analyzing the correlation between positive connotations of self-reliance and negative effects of loneliness in Don Draper that we may reveal the emptiness of success when it is achieved through distance from others.

In the second sentence of the paragraph, the author is:

A. Summarizing the show

B. Setting up a contrast between Don Draper's initial representation and the reality

C. Convincing the reader of one point of view

D. Telling a story

Here, the question is a little tricky, because the answer requires reading the entire passage instead of just the second sentence mentioned. The answer is B, because the "initial perception" of Don Draper is what the author sets out to disprove in the rest of the paragraph.

Why does the author bring up Emerson's "Self Reliance" in the paragraph?

A. To expose the differences between Don Draper and Emerson
B. To provide a contrast between Don Draper and Emerson
C. To help illuminate the character of Don Draper
D. To bring in additional evidence that Don Draper is like Emerson

The correct answer is C. Answers A and B essentially say the same thing, but the author is not contrasting but comparing the two "vaunted ideals." The main point of the paragraph is not trying to prove that Don Draper is like Emerson, however, so D is also incorrect.

Two Longer Passages — Mixed Practice

George Washington, American Forefather

George Washington was born in 1732 into a Virginia planter family. His upbringing was characterized by a strict moral code whom [1] would come to define him later in life. As was common for people of his class, he also developed a body of knowledge requisite for a Virginia gentleman. In his youth, Washington pursued two intertwined interests, and they are [2] military arts and western expansion. He later joined the military and quickly rose in the ranks, becoming a lieutenant colonel in 1754. At this time, he fought the first skirmishes of what grew into the French and Indian War. The next year, as an aide to the esteemed General Edward Braddock, he escaped narrow injury [3] although four bullets ripped his coat and two horses were shot from under him.

From 1759 to the outbreak of the American Revolution, Washington managed his lands around Mount Vernon and was serving [4] in the Virginia House of Burgesses. Married to a widow, Martha Dandridge Custis, the life that Washington devoted himself was busy and happy [5]. But like his fellow plantation owners, Washington felt exploited by British merchants and encumbered by British regulations. As the quarrel with the mother country grew, he moderately but firmly voiced [6] his resistance to the restrictions.

When the Second Continental Congress assembled in Philadelphia in May 1775, Washington one of the Virginia delegates, [7] was elected Commander in Chief of the Continental Army. On July 3, 1775, at Cambridge, Massachusetts, he took command of his ill-trained troops and embarked upon a war that was to last six long years [8]. He realized early that the best strategy was to harass the British. He was steadfast in his strategy, but the superior might of the British army forced he and his men to fall back slowly. Ever a resilient commander, though, Washington used these retreats as occasions to strike unexpectedly. Finally in 1781, with the aid of French allies, they [9] forced the surrender of the British General Cornwallis at Yorktown, Virginia.

After the war, Washington wanted nothing more than to retire to his fields at Mount Vernon. But he soon realized that the Articles of Confederation, the United States governing principles [10], were not functioning well. So, along with other prominent, American leaders [11], he became an important force in the steps leading to the Constitutional Convention at Philadelphia in 1787. When the new Constitution was ratified, <u>unanimously elected president was Washington [12]</u>.

He did not infringe upon the policy-making powers that he felt the Constitution gave Congress. But during his time in office, the determination of foreign policy became a Presidential concern. When the French Revolution led to a major war between France and England, Washington refused to accept the recommendations of either his Secretary of State Thomas Jefferson, who was pro-French, or his Secretary of the Treasury Alexander Hamilton, who was pro-British. Rather, he insisted upon a neutral course until the United States could grow stronger following the Revolutionary War. Washington served two terms as president. In his Farewell Address, he urged his countrymen to reject excessive party spirit and geographical distinctions. In foreign affairs, he warned against long-term alliances. To this day, Washington's <u>confidence, resilience, and, intelligence, [13]</u> make him a model for all future presidents.

1. **A.** NO CHANGE
   B. who
   C. that
   D. where

2. **A.** NO CHANGE
   B. interests:
   C. interests, which are
   D. interests, being

3. **A.** NO CHANGE
   B. escaped wide injury
   C. narrowly escaped injury
   D. escaped narrowly an injury

4. **A.** NO CHANGE
   B. served
   C. had been serving
   D. would have served

5. **A.** NO CHANGE
   B. Washington devoted himself to a busy and happy life
   C. happiness and business were Washington's devotions
   D. the life to which Washington devoted himself was busy and happy

6. **A.** NO CHANGE
   B. he voiced his moderate and firm
   C. his voice, moderate and firm,
   D. his voice was moderate and firm

7. **A.** NO CHANGE
   B. Washington one of the Virginia delegates
   C. Washington, one, of the Virginia delegates,
   D. Washington, one of the Virginia delegates,

8. **A.** NO CHANGE
   B. last six, long years
   C. lasted six long years
   D. be continuing for six long years

9. **A.** NO CHANGE
   B. we
   C. he
   D. one

10. **A.** NO CHANGE
    B. the United States' governing principles
    C. governing principles written by the United States
    D. principles of the United States, for government

11. **A.** NO CHANGE
    B. American, prominent leaders
    C. prominent American leaders
    D. leaders that are American and prominent

12. **A.** NO CHANGE
    B. Washington was unanimously elected president
    C. the president became Washington
    D. the person who was elected president was Washington

13. **A.** NO CHANGE
    B. confidence resilience, and intelligence
    C. confidence resilience and intelligence
    D. confidence, resilience, and intelligence

Questions 14 and 15 ask about the preceding passage as a whole.

14. For the sake of logic and coherence, Paragraph 3 should be placed:

    A. where it is now
    B. before Paragraph 2
    C. before Paragraph 5
    D. at the end of the passage

15. Suppose the writer had chosen to write an essay that describes George Washington's ascent to the presidency of the United States. Would this essay fulfill the writer's goal?

    A. No, because it spends the majority of the passage discussing his military career.
    B. No, because it is more concerned with the development of the United States than with George Washington himself.
    C. Yes, because it describes the events in Washington's life that laid the groundwork for his political career.
    D. Yes, because it demonstrates what an inspiring leader Washington was during the Revolutionary War.

Answers

1. C
2. B
3. C
4. B
5. B
6. A
7. D
8. A
9. C
10. B
11. C
12. B
13. D
14. A
15. C

Vacation in Hawaii

Surfing is a <u>wonderfully invigorating activity [1]</u> for people of any age. It can be somewhat difficult to get used to at first, but once one has a solid grasp of the skills, it becomes a fascinating, almost addictive hobby. It is no surprise given its geographic location that Hawaii is home to some of the world's best surfing. Each island in the Hawaii island chain has <u>it's [2]</u> own unique surfing attributes: Maui's relatively calm waves lend themselves to low-stakes practice sessions for beginners, while the mammoth waves of O'ahu are for experts only. The Banzai <u>Pipeline perhaps the most famous surfing region in the world, [3]</u> is home to annual surf competitions hosted by Volcom and Hurley. No matter the skill level, Hawaii will be able to take care of the average tourist's surfing needs.

Hawaii is a series of islands in the middle of the Pacific Ocean that, in 1959, became the 50th state to join the American union. Since then, <u>it is become [4]</u> a foremost tourist destination not only for Americans, but for people from around the globe, too. Hawaii boasts so many varied landscapes <u>but [5]</u> there is really never a dull moment on its shores. From the staggering heights of Mauna Kea <u>and [6]</u> the calm, pristine waters of Maui, Hawaii is unique in that it can satisfy almost any kind of travel craving. No matter a traveler's interest — whether it be hiking, swimming, cliff-diving, or relaxing — Hawaii will be able to provide. Here are a few of my favorite things to do in Hawaii.

After several hours of surfing, one inevitably gets hungry and surfing cannot be continued [7] unless that hunger is satisfied. Thankfully, Hawaii has a myriad of treats to satisfy those cravings. My favorite of all of Hawaii's delicacies [8] is definitely the acai bowl. The acai bowl has many ingredients, but is actually fairly simple to make. A mixture of acai berries, blueberries, and blackberries is poured into a blender and pureed into a thick paste. A handful of granola, in most acai bowls, had been placed [9] at the bottom of the bowl, and is then covered by this paste. Once the mixture has settled, more granola is poured over the top, followed by slices of apple, banana, coconut shavings, and a generous drizzle of honey.

Coincidentally, most of the best acai bowls can be found near the base of many of Hawaii's mountains. So, after that berry mixture and granola is all safely inside your stomach, why not venture skyward on a hike? Hawaii's mountains, like the rest of its landscapes, varied [10] in texture and climate. The mountains on O'ahu's north shore are rugged and grassy; if you hike there paths [11] all the way to completion, you will emerge onto a gorgeous westward-facing vista. On Hawaii island (known colloquially as "The Big Island"), Mount Mauna Kea rises into the stratosphere, topping out at 13,803 feet above sea level. This is no casual hike: approach [12] it only if you have the necessary equipment, strategy, and skill.

After a long day of physical exertion, my favorite thing to do is to sit down for a nice, relaxing dinner. Thanks to the bevy of sea creatures that live in proximity to the Hawaiian island chain, many of Hawaii's islands are home to world-class seafood restaurants. Sushi is particularly popular on the islands, both because fish is readily available and because Hawaii enjoys much Japanese culinary and cultural influence. If you are partial to Japanese food of any kind, you will probably feel right at home in Hawaii! Be careful, though, because some of Hawaii's abundant sea life can actually turn out to be dangerous! If not prepared correctly, sea urchin, one of Hawaii's most common restaurant offerings, are [13] poisonous. But, if cooked through, it can also be one of Hawaiian cuisine's most delicious dishes.

1. **A.** NO CHANGE
   B. wonderfully, invigorating activity
   C. wonderfully, invigoratingly activity
   D. activity that is wonderful and invigorating

2. **A.** NO CHANGE
   B. its
   C. their
   D. it is

3. **A.** NO CHANGE
   B. Pipeline perhaps the most famous surfing region in the world
   C. Pipeline, perhaps, the most famous surfing region in the world,
   D. Pipeline, perhaps the most famous surfing region in the world,

4. **A.** NO CHANGE
   B. it has become
   C. it will become
   D. it did become

5. **A.** NO CHANGE
   B. which
   C. that
   D. where

6. **A.** NO CHANGE
   B. to
   C. but
   D. where

7. **A.** NO CHANGE
   B. surfing, it must be stopped,
   C. cannot continue surfing
   D. stopping surfing is necessary

8. **A.** NO CHANGE
   B. delicacy
   C. delicacies'
   D. delicacy's

Copyright © **2016**

9. **A.** NO CHANGE
   B. was
   C. will have been
   D. is

10. **A.** NO CHANGE
    B. will have varied
    C. are likely to vary
    D. vary

11. **A.** NO CHANGE
    B. paths that are theirs
    C. their paths
    D. the paths there

12. **A.** NO CHANGE
    B. no casual hike, approach
    C. no casual hike approach
    D. no casual hike, which should be approached

13. **A.** NO CHANGE
    B. can be
    C. will have been
    D. are going to be

Questions 14 and 15 ask about the preceding passage as a whole.

14. For the sake of logic and coherence, Paragraph 2 should be placed:
   A. where it is now.
   B. before Paragraph 1.
   C. before Paragraph 4.
   D. at the end of the passage.

15. Suppose the writer had chosen to write an essay that acts as a surfer's guide to Hawaii. Would this essay fulfill the writer's goal?

    A. No, because it also covers other topics that surfers probably would not care about very much.

    B. No, because it does not discuss specific locations for surfers to explore.

    C. Yes, because it provides information on the history of surfing culture in Hawaii.

    D. Yes, because it demonstrates how great the surfing is in many different parts of Hawaii.

Answers

1. A
2. B
3. D
4. B
5. C
6. B
7. C
8. A
9. D
10. D
11. C
12. A
13. B
14. B
15. A

12—Grammar Cheat Sheet

By this time, you should be feeling pretty good about the grammar rules presented so far. You might want to just stand back for a moment, take stock in what you've learned and contemplate the Big Picture. So here are the rules — and sub-rules — teased out individually and presented in a nutshell for easy access:

Apostrophes

Concept: Use apostrophes in order to indicate possession.

- **singular** — The family's vacation took place in June.
- **plural** — The families' vacation took place in June.
- **none** — The dog ate its food.

Semicolons and Colons

Concept: Use a semicolon between two independent sentences. Comma splice.

- **wrong** — San Francisco is a small city with a large population, this results in a great deal of traffic congestion.
- **correct** — San Francisco is a small city with a large population; this results in a great deal of traffic congestion.

Concept: Use a colon to introduce lists or to augment an initial sentence (list of one).

- **lists** — The President uses a variety of different vehicles to travel: boats, planes, helicopters, and cars.
- **list of one** — The President often flies on planes: the fleet owned by the Federal Government is particularly fast.

Commas and Dashes

Concept: Use commas to separate lists, subordinate sentence details, insert parenthetical elements, introduce quotes, and precede FANBOYS.

- **lists** — I went to the store to buy coffee, tea, and milk.

Copyright © 2016

- **subordination** — Leaking oil, the car was fixed by the mechanic.
- **parenthetical expressions** — FDR, the 32nd president of the United States, died in 1945.
- **appositive** — F. Scott Fitzgerald wrote *The Great Gatsby,* a novel with an intentionally ironic title.

Misplaced Modifiers

Concept: The first noun after the comma must refer back to the action described.

- **wrong** — Leaking oil, the mechanic fixed the car.
- **correct** — Leaking oil, the car was fixed by the mechanic.

Pronoun Problems

Concept: — Get directly to the point; avoid unnecessary or vague pronouns. Be specific.

- **wrong** — When she fell down the rabbit hole, she entered a world of illusion
- **correct** — When Alice fell down the rabbit hole, she entered a world of illusion

Concept: — Subjects and subject pronouns never follow prepositions.

- **wrong** — for you and I, between you and he, with you and she, about you and they, etc. etc.
- **correct** — for you and ME, between you and him, with you and her, about you and them

Parallel Structure

Concept: — Keep nouns in parallel and verbs in parallel; don't mix the two.

- **wrong** — Mary studies history, literature and likes to paint
- **correct** — Mary studies history, literature and painting

Concept: — Conjunctions should be parallel.

- **wrong** —The judge not only sentenced the prisoner to life he also confiscated his property.
- **correct** — The judge **not only** sentenced the prisoner to life **but also** confiscated his property.

Concept: — Mistaken identity: compare like nouns.

- **wrong** — The weather in California is better than Canada
- **correct** — The weather in California is better **than the weather** in Canada

Subject/Verb Agreement

Concept: Singular subjects need singular verbs; plural subjects need plural verbs

Corollary: Delete prepositional phrases between the subject and verb.

- **wrong** — The harmful effects of saturated fat on the arterial system is well known.
- **correct** — The harmful **effects** of saturated fat on the arterial system **are** well known.

Avoid Alien Beings

Concept: For SAT/ACT grammar, avoid the use of *being*.

- **wrong** — Until being nominated for an award, the actor was a virtual unknown.
- **correct** — Until **he was** nominated for an award, the actor was a virtual unknown.

Shortest Point

Concept: For SAT/ACT grammar, shorter is almost always better.

Exception: Parallel structure sometimes requires more words for consistency.

- **longer** — Kate had finished washing the dishes and then she took out the trash.
- **shorter** — When Kate finished washing the dishes, she took out the trash.

Who vs. Whom

Concept: Use *who* when the secondary verb in the sentence needs a subject. Use *whom* when the secondary verb has a subject.

- **who** — Susan, who loves dogs, volunteers at the local SPCA.
- **whom** — Susan, whom dogs love, volunteers at the local SPCA.

Writer's Goal

Concept: Look at the passage as a whole to determine the most logical placement of paragraphs, the most consistent use of transitions, and the most apt description of the author's purpose in writing.

Part II Readings

This section combines all the rules together in a couple of academically advanced, culturally relevant reading passage from major news media. Modifications to the original text have been made to highlight the grammar points covered so far in this book.

Without any external prompting, and with your new-found grammar skills, you should be able to spot and correct the various mistakes built into the text.

Copyright © 2016

A—The Myth of Big Bad Gluten

This article has been edited to include grammatical mistakes, none of which are the fault of the author.

The Myth of Big Bad Gluten
by Moises Velasquez-Manoff, with permission from the New York Times

As many as one in three Americans try [1] to avoid gluten, a protein found in wheat, barley and rye. Gluten-free menus, gluten-free labels and gluten-free guests at summer dinners have show up in great numbers [2].

Some of the anti-glutenists argue that we haven't eaten wheat for long enough to adapt to it as a specie's [3]. Agriculture began just 12,000 years ago, not enough time for our bodies, who [4] evolved over millions of years, primarily in Africa, to adjust. Accordingly [5], we're intrinsically hunter-gatherers, not bread-eaters. If exposed to gluten, some of us will develop celiac disease or gluten intolerance.

Most of these assertions however, [6] are contradicted by significant evidence and distract us from our actual problem, an [7] immune system that has become overly sensitive. [8]

Considering [9] how some populations have adapted to milk consumption over time. We can digest lactose, a sugar in milk, as infants, but many stop producing the enzyme that breaks it down, called lactase — [10] in adulthood. For these "lactose intolerant" people, drinking milk can cause bloating and diarrhea. Coping with lactase intolerance, a trait called lactase persistence was evolved by milk-drinking populations. [11]

Milk-producing animals were first domesticated about the same time as wheat in the Middle East. As the custom of dairying spread, lactase persistence between [12] herders also did. What surprises scientists today is just how recently, and how completely, that trait has spread in some populations. Few Scandinavian hunter-gatherers living 5,400 year's [13] ago had lactase persistence genes, for example. Today, most Scandinavians do.

Copyright © 2016

Here's the lesson: Adaptation to a new food stuff can occur <u>quick [14]</u> — in a few millenniums in this case. So if it happened with milk, why not with wheat?

"If eating wheat was so bad for us, it's hard to imagine that populations that <u>eat [15]</u> it would have tolerated it for 10,000 years," Sarah A. Tishkoff, a geneticist at the University of Pennsylvania who studies lactase persistence, told me.

For Dr. Bana <u>Jabri, director of research at the University of Chicago Celiac Disease Center, it's [16]</u> the genetics of celiac disease that contradict the argument that wheat is intrinsically toxic.

Active celiac disease can cause severe health problems, from stunting and osteoporosis <u>and [17]</u> miscarriage. It strikes a relatively small number of people — just around 1 percent of the population. Yet given the significant costs to fitness for us, <u>you'd [18]</u> anticipate that the genes associated with celiac would be gradually removed from the gene pool of those eating wheat.

A few years ago, Dr. Jabri and the population geneticist Luis B. Barreiro tested that assumption and discovered precisely the opposite. Not only were celiac-associated genes abundant in the Middle Eastern populations <u>who's [19]</u> ancestors first domesticated wheat; some celiac-linked variants showed evidence of having spread in recent millenniums.

People who had them, in other words, had some advantage compared with those who didn't.

Questions

1. NO CHANGE
   B. tries
   C. have tried
   D. had tried

2. A. NO CHANGE
   B. become ever larger
   C. proliferated
   D. gotten bigger

3. A. NO CHANGE
   B. specie's
   C. species'
   D. species

4. A. NO CHANGE
   B. which
   C. that
   D. whose

5. A. NO CHANGE
   B. According to it
   C. According to this theory
   D. In accordance with the idea

6. A. NO CHANGE
   B. ; however,
   C. , however,
   D. , however

7. A. NO CHANGE
   B. ; an
   C. : an
   D. an

8. The author is considering adding this sentence: Wheat was first domesticated in southeastern Anatolia perhaps 11,000 years ago. Should the

sentence be added?

   A. No, because it presents the author's opinion rather than historical fact

   B. No, because it detracts from the narrative flow of the passage

   C. Yes, because it acts as a transition to the following paragraph

   D. Yes, because it lends geographical perspective to the narrative

9. **A.** NO CHANGE
   B. Having considered
   C. Consider
   D. To consider

10. **A.** NO CHANGE
    B. called lactase,
    C. , called lactase —
    D. — called lactase —

11. **A.** NO CHANGE
    B. a trait called lactase persistence had evolved by milk-drinking populations.
    C. milk-drinking populations evolved a trait called lactase persistence.
    D. milk-drinking evolved.

12. **A.** NO CHANGE
    B. in between
    C. among
    D. around

13. **A.** NO CHANGE
    B. years
    C. years'
    D. year

14. **A.** NO CHANGE
    B. quicker
    C. very quick
    D. quickly

15. **A.** NO CHANGE
    B. eaten

C. had ate

D. ate

16. **A.** NO CHANGE

   B. Jabri, director, of research at the University of Chicago Celiac Disease Center it's

   C. Jabri, director of research, at the University of Chicago, Celiac Disease Center, it's

   D. Jabri, director of research at the University of Chicago Celiac Disease Center, its

17. **A.** NO CHANGE

   B. but

   C. yet

   D. to

18. **A.** NO CHANGE

   B. we'd

   C. you would

   D. we would have

19. **A.** NO CHANGE

   B. who is

   C. whom

   D. whose

Copyright © **2016**

Answers

1. B
2. C
3. D
4. B
5. A
6. C
7. A
8. B
9. C
10. D
11. C
12. C
13. B
14. D
15. D
16. A
17. D
18. B
19. D

B — Why Teenagers Act Crazy

This article has been edited to include grammatical mistakes, none of which are the fault of the author.

Why Teenagers Act Crazy

by Richard A. Friedman with permission from the New York Times

Adolescence is practically synonymous in our culture with risk taking, emotional drama and all forms of outlandish behavior. Until very recently, the widely accepted explanation for adolescent angst <u>had been [1]</u> psychological. Developmentally, teenagers face a number of social and emotional <u>challenges: like [2]</u> starting to separate from their parents, getting accepted into a peer group and figuring out <u>there [3]</u> place in life. It doesn't take a psychoanalyst to realize that these are anxiety-provoking transitions.

But there is a darker side to adolescence that, until now, was poorly understood: a <u>surge, during teenage years in [4]</u> anxiety and fearfulness. Largely because of a quirk of brain development, adolescents, on average, <u>experiences [5]</u> more anxiety and fear and have a harder time learning how not to be afraid than either children or adults.

Different regions and circuits of the brain mature at very different rates. It turns out that the brain circuit for processing fear — the amygdala — is precocious and develops way ahead of the prefrontal cortex, <u>that is the seat [6]</u> of reasoning and executive control. This means that adolescents have a brain that is wired with an enhanced capacity for fear and anxiety, <u>and [7]</u> is relatively underdeveloped when it comes to calm reasoning.

That reward center drives much of teenagers' risky behavior <u>[8]</u>. You may wonder why, <u>if adolescent's [9]</u> have such enhanced capacity for anxiety, they are such novelty seekers and risk takers. It would seem that the two traits are at odds. The answer, in part, is that the brain's reward <u>center, being just like [10]</u> its fear circuit, matures earlier than the prefrontal cortex.

The brain-development lag has huge implications for how we think about anxiety, stress, and how we treat it [11]. It suggests that as an anxious adolescent, one may not be very responsive to psychotherapy who's goal [12] is to teach you to be unafraid. As a psychiatrist, many adults with various anxiety disorders have been treated by me [13], nearly all of whom trace the origin of the problem to their teenage years.

Of course, most adolescents do not develop anxiety disorders, but acquire the skill to modulate their fear as their prefrontal cortex matures in young adulthood, at around age 25. But up to 20 percent of adults in the United States experience a diagnosable anxiety disorder. The prevalence of anxiety disorders and risky behaviors, both of whom [14] reflect this developmental disjunction in the brain, has [15] been relatively steady, which suggests to me that the biological contribution is very significant.

The amygdala is a region buried deep beneath the cortex that is critical in evaluating and responding to fear. It sends and receive [16] connections to our prefrontal cortex alerting us to danger even before you have had [17] time to really think about it.

Adolescents are not just carefree novelty seekers and risk takers; they [18] are uniquely vulnerable to anxiety and have a hard time learning to be unafraid of passing dangers. Parents have to realize that adolescent anxiety is to be expected, and to comfort their teenagers — and themselves — by reminding them [19] that they will grow up and out of it soon enough.

118

Questions

1. **A.** NO CHANGE
   B. were
   C. has been
   D. having been

2. **A.** NO CHANGE
   B. challenges — like
   C. challenges like,
   D. challenges like

3. **A.** NO CHANGE
   B. their
   C. they're
   D. which

4. **A.** NO CHANGE
   B. surge, during teenage years, in
   C. surge, during, teenage years in
   D. surge during teenage years in

5. **A.** NO CHANGE
   B. experience
   C. has experienced
   D. had experienced

6. **A.** NO CHANGE
   B. which is the seat
   C. that is the seat,
   D. , who is the seat

7. **A.** NO CHANGE
   B. but
   C. that
   D. which

8. Where would this sentence best be placed? *That reward center drives much of teenagers' risky behavior.*

    A. NO CHANGE
    B. after the first sentence
    C. after the second sentence
    D. at the end of the paragraph

9. **A.** NO CHANGE
    B. if adolescents
    C. if, adolescents
    D. if, adolescents,

10. **A.** NO CHANGE
    B. center, just like
    C. center just like
    D. center being just like

11. **A.** NO CHANGE
    B. anxiety stress, and how we treat it
    C. anxiety, stress, and treatment
    D. anxiety, stress and, treatment

12. **A.** NO CHANGE
    B. that's goal
    C. which goal
    D. whose goal

13. **A.** NO CHANGE
    B. I have treated many adults with anxiety disorders
    C. I have treated with anxiety disorders many adults
    D. many adults have been treated by me with anxiety disorders

14. **A.** NO CHANGE
    B. both of which
    C. both of that
    D. that both

15. **A.** NO CHANGE
    B. would of
    C. have
    D. has had

16. **A.** NO CHANGE
    B. send and receives
    C. sends and receives
    D. having sent, receives

17. **A.** NO CHANGE
    B. you've had
    C. we've have
    D. we have had

18. **A.** NO CHANGE
    B. risk, takers, they
    C. risk takers, they
    D. risk takers they

19. **A.** NO CHANGE
    B. their parents
    C. their children
    D. the people

Answers

1. C
2. D
3. A
4. B
5. B
6. D
7. A
8. D
9. B
10. B
11. C
12. D
13. B
14. B
15. C
16. C
17. D
18. A
19. C

C — 2b or Not 2b

This article has been edited to include grammatical mistakes, none of which are the fault of the author.

2b or Not 2b

by David Crystal, with permission from the author

Last year, in a newspaper article headed "I h8 txt msgs: How texting is wrecking our language", John Humphry's [1] argued that texters are "vandals which [2] are doing to our language the same that [3] Genghis Khan did to his neighbors 800 years ago. They are destroying it; [4] pillaging our punctuation, savaging our sentences, and raping our vocabulary. They must be stopped."

As a new variety of language, texting has been condemned as being [5] "textese", "slanguage", a "digital virus". According to John Sutherland of University College London, writing in this paper in 2002, it is "bleak, bald, and sad shorthand. Texting has been [6] penmanship for illiterates."

Ever since the arrival of printing - thought to be the invention of the devil because it would put false opinions into people's minds, [7] people have been arguing that new technology must have [8] disastrous consequences for language. Scares [9] accompanied the introduction of the telegraph, telephone, and broadcasting. But has there ever been a linguistic phenomenon which has aroused such curiosity, excitement and enthusiasm all at once as texting? And with such a short space of time. Less than a decade ago, hardly anyone had heard of it.

The idea of a point-to-point short message service, (or SMS) [10] began to be discussed as part of the development of the Global System for Mobile Communications network in the mid-1980s. However; [11] it wasn't until the early 90s that phone companies started to develop its commercial possibilities. Text communicated by pagers were replaced by text messages, at first only 20 characters in length. The average number of texts per GSM customer in 1995 was 0.4 per month; by the end of 2000 it was still only 35.

*Copyright © **2016***

The slow start, it seems, was because the <u>companies' [12]</u> had trouble working out reliable ways of charging for the new service. But once procedures were in place, texting rocketed. In the UK, in 2001, 12.2bn text messages were sent. This had doubled by 2004, and was forecast to be 45bn in 2007. On Christmas Day alone in 2006, over 205m texts <u>had gone out.[13]</u> World figures went from 17bn in 2000 to 250bn in 2001. They passed a trillion in 2005. Text messaging generated around $70bn in 2005. That's more than three times as much as all Hollywood box office returns that year.[14]

People think that the written language seen on mobile phone screens is new and alien, but all the popular beliefs about texting are wrong. <u>Its [15]</u> graphic distinctiveness is not a new phenomenon, nor is its use restricted to the young. There is increasing evidence that it helps rather than <u>was hindered by[16]</u> literacy. [1]And only a very tiny part of it uses a distinctive orthography. [2] A trillion text messages might seem a lot. [3] But when we set these alongside the multi-trillion instances of standard orthography in everyday life, they appear as no more than a few ripples on the surface of the sea of language. [4] Texting has added a new dimension to language use, but its long-term impact is negligible.[17]

Questions

1. **A.** NO CHANGE
   B. Humphryie's
   C. Humphrys
   D. Humphrys'

2. **A.** NO CHANGE
   B. that
   C. who
   D. whose

3. **A.** NO CHANGE
   B. that
   C. that which
   D. what

4. **A.** NO CHANGE
   B. it
   C. it:
   D. it,

5. **A.** NO CHANGE
   B. like
   C. as
   D. in accordance with the idea that

6. **A.** NO CHANGE
   B. was being
   C. had been
   D. is

7. **A.** NO CHANGE
   B. , thought to be the invention of the devil because it would put false opinions into people's minds —
   C. , thought to be the invention of the devil because it would put false opinions into people's minds,
   D. thought to be the invention of the devil because it would put false opinions into people's minds —

Copyright © **2016**

8. **A.** NO CHANGE
    B. should have
    C. could have
    D. would have

9. **A.** NO CHANGE
    B. Scare's
    C. Scares were
    D. Scaring was

10. **A.** NO CHANGE
    B. (or SMS),
    C. (SMS)
    D. Short Message Service

11. **A.** NO CHANGE
    B. However,
    C. However
    D. However --

12. **A.** NO CHANGE
    B. companie's,
    C. company
    D. companies

13. **A.** NO CHANGE
    B. were gone out.
    C. were gone.
    D. went out.

14. The author is considering adding this sentence to the end of this paragraph: "Most of the text users were single white males in their 20s."

   A. No, because it misreprensents a variety of ethnic groups.
   B. No, because it detracts from the narrative flow of the passage.
   C. Yes, because it acts as a transition to the following paragraph.
   D. Yes, because it lends popular support to the narrative.

15. A. NO CHANGE
   B. Its'
   C. It is
   D. It's

16. A. NO CHANGE
   B. hinders
   C. hindered
   D. was being hindered by

17. Which is the most logical place for the following sentence: "In the final analysis, it is not a disaster."

   A. after sentence (1)
   B. after sentence (2)
   C. after sentence (3)
   D. after sentence (4)

Answers

1. C
2. C
3. D
4. D
5. C
6. D
7. C
8. D
9. A
10. C
11. B
12. D
13. D
14. B
15. A
16. B
17. D

D—Becoming Americans

This article is from a newspaper journalist who, as you might expect, has an excellent command of grammar and punctuation. However, even excellent writers may, on occasion, err. Your job in this section is twofold:

1. Specify *why* the selected entries in the passage are correct
2. Spot the one, admittedly small, *error* in the piece

Note: In this passage, the writer avoids the Harvard comma, a personal (and legit) style choice. No problem.

Becoming Americans — and What It Means

by Vanessa Hua, with permission from the author
San Francisco Chronicle, 2016-07

Almost a year ago, [1]Ahmad, his wife and their son and daughter celebrated their first Fourth of July in America by going to the parade in Pleasant Hill— [2] a friendly small-town bash <u>where cheerleaders caper, local dignitaries ride in classic cars, and spectators decked out in red, white and blue wave little flags. [3]</u>

After applying for asylum, the Iraqi family was still getting its bearings. Somewhere in the crowd, Ahmad lost his wallet. He and his wife frantically searched for <u>it; [4] replacing his identification cards while getting settled in a new country would have been arduous.</u>

"Thankfully, [5] some kind person found it and took it to the police station," said the gregarious 42-year-old, [6]<u>who</u> wore a polo shirt and stylish glasses. (He didn't want his last name disclosed for fear of putting his family in Iraq at risk.)

We were sitting in their cozy two-bedroom apartment while the children finished [7] <u>their</u> afternoon snack of spaghetti. Despite rising anti-Muslim sentiment in this country, [8] the family members say they feel welcome here. Every day, they work at putting down roots, and in process, become American.

Copyright © **2016**

"People in the Bay Area have shown us nothing but kindness in trying to help us out," Ahmad said. His bubbly wife, [9] Abeer, in an off-the-shoulder striped top, pushed back her wavy chestnut hair and urged me to eat the snacks [10]she'd prepared:[11] fish sticks, pasta salad, two pizzas and a pile of croissants.

The family is [12] among the millions who have fled war and other violence in the Middle East. In 2014, the United States accepted 19,769 refugees from Iraq,[13] and 629 were granted asylum. (Both programs offer refuge to people who have been persecuted or have a well-founded fear of persecution; [14] refugees refer to people who apply from outside the United States, while those seeking asylum do so here.) According to the U.N. refugee agency, more than 65 million people worldwide were displaced last year, [15] a record high.

Ahmad sympathizes with [16] families now making the treacherous journey across the Mediterranean Sea. Historically, refugee crossings rise during the summer months.

"I feel what they feel. They want to lead a normal life. They don't want to worry about their kids getting bombed. They want to go to work every day and feel their house is safe," he said. "Nobody is choosing to change all their life without a reason. They have no guarantee for what they will do next, but they have to take the risk."

For more than a decade, [17] he had been working as an architect in the United Arab Emirates, where he met his wife, also a native of Iraq. But with his employer set to shut down, he would lose his Emirates residency permit and his family would be forced to go back to Iraq.

As returnees, they would have been targeted by the Islamic State. "These people want to demolish the history of thousands of years, wipe up everything, and take us back to the Stone Age,"[18] he said.

They decided to travel to the United States [19] and seek asylum. Though the upheaval in Iraq has scattered his family and his [20] wife's to Canada and the Emirates over the decades, they keep in touch via the Internet. He worries about those in Iraq, struggling and in peril, and [21] able to make only sporadic contact. They are vivid in his memories and in the precious black-and-white photos scanned by his sister and shared among siblings.

Ahmad and his family had to leave most of their [22] possessions behind to come here, joining the ranks of "the homeless, tempest-tost" immortalized in the poem engraved on a plaque on the Statue of Liberty's pedestal. Their asylum application is pending. Eventually, they want to apply for green cards and U.S. citizenship.

To help their children fit in, [23] he and his wife volunteered at their elementary school. Ahmad corrected spelling and grammar and stapled papers, whatever the teacher asked of him, while Abeer joined field trips. Their 6-year-old daughter loves to draw and their 8-year-old son is a fan of "Minecraft."

After getting his work permit, Ahmad [24]worked as a supervisor at an electronics shop, but continued looking for a position that matched his experience. San Francisco's Upwardly Global — which provides training and support for skilled, college-educated immigrants — [25] set up a few interviews.

Answers

1. Correct — A comma is needed to separate the compound subject.

2. Correct — A dash is as good as a comma when ending a sentence.

3. Correct — Notice the parallel verbs: caper, ride, and wave.

4. Correct — Tricky. As we know, a semicolon connects two independent sentences. In this case, *replacing his identification cards while getting settled in a new country* **is** the subject, followed by the verb form *would have been*.

5. Correct — A comma is used as a transition to introduce the sentence.

6. Correct — *Who* is a subject pronoun preceding the verb *wore*.

7. Correct — *Their* is the correct possessive pronoun.

8. Correct — A comma is needed to separate the introductory phrase from the main sentence.

9. Correct — Commas are needed to set off *Abeer* from the main sentence.

10. Correct — *She'd* is the correct contraction for *she would*.

11. Correct — A colon is used to introduce a list.

12. Correct — Among is used for three or more. Between is used for two.

13. Correct — A comma is used to separate two independent sentences connected by *and*. Fanboy rule.

14. Correct — A semicolon is used to connect two independent sentences.

15. Correct — A comma is used with an appositive to provide extra information to the end of the sentence.

16. Correct — Families is a plural noun. No possessive punctuation is required.

17. Correct — Nice use of the past perfect continuous: *had been working*.

18. Correct — Notice that the comma is inside — not outside — the quotes.

19. Correct — Compound verbs don't require a comma.

20. Correct — Apostrophe denotes possession.

21. Wrong — The comma before *and* makes the sentence seem like there's a

compound verb, which is clearly not the case. This violates parallel structure. To see this more clearly, eliminate the extra information *struggling and in peril* then try reading the sentence like this: *He worries about those in Iraq, and able to make only sporadic contact.* The sentence should read: *He worries about those in Iraq, struggling and in peril, and **is** able to make only sporadic contact.* Now the verb forms (*worries, is able*) are parallel. Alternatively, the sentence could be re-written like this: *He worries about those in Iraq, struggling and in peril and able to make only sporadic contact.*

22. Correct — No apostrophe is needed.

23. Correct — *He* is a subject pronoun.

24. Correct — Ahmad is the correct subject, the person getting the work permit. This sentence is not *leaking oil.*

25. Correct — Dashes can be used like commas to seperate extra information out from the sentence.

Copyright © **2016**

Made in the USA
Coppell, TX
09 February 2023

12490458R00077